PARENTS, ARE YOU READY?

**THE PRACTICAL GUIDE TO LAUNCHING
A SUCCESSFUL HIGH SCHOOL STUDENT
THE 15-STEP ROADMAP**

KIM DUCKWORTH

Publishing Services provided by Paper Raven Books LLC

Printed in the United States of America

First Printing, 2022

Paperback ISBN= 979-8-9850058-0-6
Hardback ISBN= 979-8-9850058-1-3

For my dazzling, treasured daughters,
Heather, Angela, and Claire,
and my cherished husband, David

"…Guide them along the way, children will listen

Children will look to you for which way to turn

To learn what to be.

Careful before you say, 'Listen to me.'

Children will listen."

—Stephen Sondheim, *Into the Woods*

TABLE OF CONTENTS

INTRODUCTION

What you will find in this book may be controversial in many circles today. It goes against the prevailing "do less, get more" message that has permeated our culture. There are an abundance of self-help gurus who hail the virtue of getting more by doing less, advocating for shortened workweeks and telling people to take it easy and not work so hard. Doing less and making more is a sentiment that plays well into three of humankind's most lethal characteristics: laziness, greediness, and ignorance. It takes effort to change the flawed ideas that stem from these three foibles. As parents, we need to teach and show our children the importance of having a strong work ethic and trying…always trying…our best.

We are told that we can do less and be a superstar. Unfortunately, that is NOT what I have observed or experienced over 12 years as the owner of Scottsdale Education Center (SEC), a college preparatory center I owned with my husband, David. Success requires an immense amount of effort and commitment. I have read high school students' resumes that literally took my breath away. How did they have time to sleep with that level of achievement? And, even more amazingly, how in the world

1

do they manage to keep a big smile on their faces despite all the challenges they face? Well, they smile because of the self-satisfaction that comes with true accomplishment. I have worked with students who have raised thousands of dollars for community service organizations, some of which they themselves had founded, and who have won national and even international awards. By the edict of some, these kids should have been miserable. In the eyes of the do-lessers, accomplishment is often seen as a sin. But that is not what I have seen. Accomplishment has created invaluable opportunities for these children and has set the stage for them to thrive in high school and beyond. In working with thousands of students, I have learned one very important lesson: never underestimate what a child can do even while they are still in high school.

The nationally recruited star athletes who love chemistry, dancers who crave math, and artists who ace physics do exist. They were taught to be curious, to read, to think. They have worked to find their passion, but not to the exclusion of all else. They had parents who made them...yes, made them...go deep, be curious and well rounded, and have an academic passion as well as a life passion. They had parents who helped them identify what they were good at and loved to learn about, to explore what fascinated them. They had parents who believed in them and encouraged them to work hard to get what they wanted, not to sit back and be upset when they didn't get the low-hanging fruit. Training, rehearsing, and doing homework are all necessary to get better. Doing less will not make you better at something. You have to DO something. As adults, we know that. Now, don't get me wrong. Everyone deserves down time...a vacation. But, it has to be earned. We need to make sure we teach that to our children and show them how to do it.

Your child learns from you every day. What you say and what you do shows them what you value. Make sure you are investing in them...helping them find their weirdness (uniqueness), their superpower, their curiosity and passion. They will know if you are...or if you aren't.

"Sisu"

At the age of 16, my grandmother Mary came to the United States by herself on a boat from Finland. She did not speak a word of English, and all she had with her was a well-worn and underlined Finnish Bible, a few clothes, and a contract for her indentured servitude as a domestic slave. She was contracted to work and live in the home of a wealthy family for five years before she could leave and be free. The only pictures I have of her in her youthful days are from when she was a teenager. In these pictures, she wears a maid's outfit. Her hands were big and rough and misshapen from accidents she had while scrubbing floors on her knees with a brush and bucket of soapy fluid. After her service was completed, she landed in the Upper Peninsula of Michigan. There, she met and married my grandfather, a coal miner who was also Finnish. He died from lung disease when Mary was pregnant with my father. She never really spoke English, and the only picture I ever saw on the walls of her house was one capturing the day she became a U.S. citizen. She drank really, really, really strong coffee...all day long...and made fish pies with the heads still on the fish as well as a heavenly bread called *nissua*. She was brave, decisive, and a survivor. Mary was a living Viking. And it was what I learned from her that precipitated me getting into my dream college and breaking a vicious family cycle of poverty and hardship.

Neither of my grandmothers graduated from high school…nor did my mother, who was married when she was 16 (the first of three marriages that ended in divorce). To the best of my knowledge, I was the first woman in my family to graduate high school, the first to go to college, the first to graduate from college, the first to graduate in three years, and the first to graduate from a highly selective college: Stanford University. I pushed myself to graduate in three years because I couldn't afford to do it in four. During my senior year of high school, I went to night school at Cal State, San Bernardino and took a full 15-unit load so that I could transfer courses. During college, I worked 20 hours per week and had to get special permission some terms to go beyond the 20 unit maximum. It was hard.

We never had much money when I was growing up. My father was a middle school history teacher, coach, and night janitor. My mother lost her job and ability to drive when she became an alcoholic. When I was 16, there were times my mother was so drunk when she came to pick me up after school that I had to take the car keys away from her and drive us both home, arguing with her in front of the school and trying to cajole her out of the driver's seat in front of friends, teachers, and administrators. When I was even younger than that, I used to get calls at 2 a.m. from bartenders who had taken my mother's keys away from her and would not let her drive home. We didn't have money for her to take a taxi home and I was too young to drive, even if there had been a car for me to drive at home, so I was tasked with watching my younger brother who was sleeping upstairs. It would often take some time to track down my father to pick her up as they were divorced and he didn't live with us (and there were no cell phones in those days). Sometimes I had to call upon older high school friends to pick her up. So, at 16, I was often in charge of myself, my 13-year-old brother, and my mother.

Every school day, I was given one dollar for lunch. Rather than spend the full amount on food, I would use half of it to buy an apple from the vending machine and put the rest in my college savings. I started working part-time the minute I turned 16 and put as much of my earnings as I could towards my college fund. We were not rich. And I say that to let you know that this book is not the brainchild of a rich, Ivy League, privileged life or some mere "idea" of what it must be like to struggle just to get by. I lived it. I share all of this with you to provide context for why I wrote this book. Education, for me, was the way to escape a vicious cycle. It freed me from a small life. As abolitionist and former slave Frederick Douglass once penned, "education is what emancipates us." Having been raised by a teacher, my brother and I understood it was expected that we would: (1) go to school always, (2) be respectful of teachers, and (3) do well in school…meaning work hard and get the best grades possible. In elementary school, we would get a dime for an A and a nickel for a B. My father, who didn't speak English until he started kindergarten, gave us a Finnish word that he had learned from his mother, Mary, that embodies what got me here today: *sisu*. I placed this as a bumper sticker on our family car and wrote my college essay on it. It means intestinal fortitude. Or, the way I would always think about it …GUTS. It is what Mary had and what I desperately aspired to live by. I would say *sisu* is in the heart of every successful parent.

I have raised three children who are grown now, but I do not claim to have been a perfect parent. In fact, I would submit to you that there is no such thing as a perfect parent. We may have good moments, but we are inevitably human. In the words of famed football coach Vince Lombardi, "Perfection is not attainable, but if we chase perfection we can catch excellence." We all bring our own backgrounds and stories into our parenting roles. What might work like a charm with one child usually will not work with another. Having three daughters who were each almost exactly two years apart, I had a tendency to think that what I would say to one would translate well to the next. But that didn't always work (perhaps, more accurately, it rarely worked).

There were some basic family mantras that I grew up with…those things that my parents would say over and over again that shaped us: to thine own self be true (Shakespeare), two wrongs don't make a right (Benjamin Rush), do your best, and *sisu*. I am sure those have inevitably creeped into my own parenting style. With the melding of my husband's parenting philosophy and mine, our family's mantras became: finish long and strong (translated by Disney lore to Nemo's always "touch the butt"), think BOLD (a spin-off of IBM's iconic THINK message emblazoned into the minds of its employees, which I picked up from my 11-year sales and marketing career at the company), and a Bible quote from Proverbs: "Trust in the Lord with all your heart" (which hopefully can be helpful to my daughters as they face adulthood and develop their own parenting styles).

So, knowing that education was instrumental in changing the trajectory of my life, David and I decided to buy an education business and ran it successfully for 12 years. Scottsdale Education Center is a college preparatory center providing tutoring services for high school and middle school students, college admission testing preparatory services, summer enrichment and remediation classes, and college admissions coaching. This book takes the concepts we learned about how students could succeed in high school and redirects those ideas to provide direction…practical direction…for the **parents** of high school students and how they can be successful.

Parents, Are You Ready?

Some of you may be thinking "I was born ready" or may feel completely prepared because you have already been through the process at least once before. But I KNOW that each child is different and that something has been going on in your household that you may not have been completely aware of. Over the past months, a "shapeshifter" has actually invaded your home and taken over your "almost" high schooler. They are being transformed before your very eyes. They now have big fears and tears, their earphones are becoming permanently attached to their heads, they listen extensively to peers, and they may be considering drinking alcohol or trying drugs. Their questionable decision-making abilities may cause them to veer in the wrong direction. You don't think they hear a thing you say and you are even sometimes on the receiving end of jeers and leers, but they need someone to cheer them on. The sheer stress and uncertainty of it all is heightened by the fact that it has been a while since you were in high school and you know at some level that it is a different time and world than when you were a teenager. So, what do you need to know now?

This book is not a theoretical or "academic" review of high school parenting. Rather, it is a practical guide based on over a decade of experience with helping parents create a plethora of options for their child. For the past decade plus, we have helped students successfully graduate from high school, nail standardized college admissions tests, successfully complete Advanced Placement (AP) and International Baccalaureate (IB) programs, college dual enrollment courses, gain attendance to elite private high schools both locally and nationally, and create a multitude of college admission options. Over the years, our center has served the needs of approximately 15,000 students from local public high schools, the top charter schools in the nation (BASIS), Great Heart Academy charter schools, elite private Catholic high schools (Brophy, Xavier, and Notre Dame Preparatory), and a variety of different online high school programs (Laurel Springs, BYU online, K12, Primavera).

Our students have represented a wide variety of academic abilities. Some had documented learning disabilities, ADD/ADHD, Asperger's, or behavioral issues that impacted their ability to learn in traditional educational environments. For some of these students, a basic study skills class was paramount. We also worked with gifted students and students who graduated with 4s and 5s in over 15 AP classes. To give you a perspective of the intensity of some of these programs, one of them has middle school students (6th, 7th, and 8th grade) taking chemistry, biology, and physics for three years before even starting high school and taking an AP world history class and test in the 8th grade. Their AP classes and tests are college-level curriculum, and their tests require advanced critical thinking skills and college-level writing abilities. Students at this middle school are expected to have reached that level five years before most of their age group. The expectation was that a 13- or 14-year-old could perform academically at the same level as an 18- or 19-year-old...and some of them did.

To say the least, we saw a WIDE variety of academic offerings and a WIDE variety of student abilities and parenting styles. Independent of the student or program, there were some key ingredients for a successful completion of those high school years that help both parents and students be successful at graduation, with success being defined as having multiple life choices available after "Pomp and Circumstance" has played. Every student is different and requires different nurturing, and your own unique knowledge of your child has to be applied as you read this book. Some of the concepts may run completely contrary to other things you have read, but at SEC we saw what worked. Other concepts are just no-nonsense, block-and-tackle parenting.

For 10 years, we offered a "How to Succeed in High School" class for rising high school freshman and sophomore students. It helped students see the big picture of the high school years. Several parents asked us to take what we knew and turn it into a class for them. That was the inspiration for this book, which is a ROADMAP of what to DO and specific actions for you to take to help your child accomplish a successful high school experience. Some parents have told me that their child's high school experience will have been successful if they make it through the four years alive, out of jail, and not pregnant. Having raised three spunky and highly successful daughters, I understand the sentiment and I know you want the best for your child.

I wrote this book to pass on what we learned working with over 15,000 high school students and their parents from a variety of backgrounds and schools. It is designed to be a real-life, practical guide for how parents can successfully maneuver those difficult high school years and create as many options as possible for their children…and for both parents and their children to remain sane in the process. I wrote this to pass on what I was taught by my living Viking grandmother about hard work, resilience, and determination. My goal is to help parents reclaim a sometimes lost vision of the importance of GUTS and the place for *sisu* in parenting.

How to Read This Book

The design of this book is to be a WORKbook. There are things that you need to DO: questions to ask, things to review, listening to be done. There are encouragements that must take place, examples that you must make to SHOW them that you are interested and paying attention to them. Here in Arizona, we frequently see bevies of quail on the street. There is always one quail parent in the lead and one at the end of a string of a newly hatched brood. The parent at the back is constantly regrouping the little ones in between to make sure they all get to where they are being led. They teach the baby quail how to cross a street, avoid rattlesnake holes, and find the best food. I have seen a string of as many as 16 little ones at a time. The very visage of a family that large is exhausting. And to further complicate things for us humans, sometimes we need to be the one in the lead and the one at the back at the same time, eyes and ears everywhere. But the thing about the quail families is they appear to try their very hardest to make sure no one…not one of the offspring… gets left behind.

Whenever I see them, I think of what a great visual reminder it is that, as parents, we need to always lead our children and keep them on track. We lead by DOING and by how we conduct ourselves every day, and we keep them on track by really understanding what they are doing every day. Be interested in them, because they are very interesting. Life for children can have huge rattlesnake holes…drugs, bullying, drinking…and we need to SHOW them how to avoid the pitfalls. A picture of a bevy of quail being led by a parent is a great visual reminder of the mindset you need to have as you read this book. Better yet, put that visual on your refrigerator or in your car.

To get the most out of this book, you need to DO the exercises with your child. They are changing right before your eyes, whether you are aware of it or not. When they are really little, you can see the physical changes daily. As they get older, the changes are still going on, but you may not have the same visual clues. Doing many of these exercises once a year can be helpful, and a student version of this workbook is coming out soon. Ultimately, though, you need to lead the discussion.

Leading doesn't mean doing it for them. I can't tell you how many times I have sat down with a student and their parent in a college admission coaching session, asked the student what it is they are thinking of studying in college, and had the student give me an answer that is obviously a huge surprise to the parent. And I can't tell you how many times I have heard the parent proclaim, "I thought you were interested in studying X, not Y." Those last two years of high school college lists, dreams, and interests can change dramatically. Most importantly, if someone asks your child that question, let them answer. Learn to lead but not smother. Help them discover who they are but not dictate who they must be.

One of the most puzzling things I had a parent do in a session, in front of their child, was to ask me if I thought they should legally change the child's last name so that they could be in a less competitive admissions pool. Their surname was unmistakably Chinese, and they did not want their child competing against other high-performing Asian students for admission. The irony was that their child had one of the most competitive profiles I had ever seen, from academics and test scores to leadership and performing arts. The child lowered her head and blushed red. Her parent had just told her that they did not think she was good enough to compete with other students. They did not think she was good enough. She heard it. I heard it. But somehow the parent didn't. Their expectations were unrealistic for ANY child. So, the other thing I would encourage you to do as you are reading this book is to listen to what you are saying to your child. Listen to what your words and actions are telling them. Look at who they are. Learn who they are. Listen to their answers. Be engaged without reliving YOUR high school or life dreams.

Let's keep in mind three specific goals for successful completion of high school:

1. Create as many "options" for your child as possible, ideally starting in middle school.
2. Help them answer the question "who are you?"
3. Use resources.

Built around these three goals, this book is divided into four parts. Part One walks you through the roadmap for preparing your child for success, including the 15 critical success factors to cultivate in middle school and high school and the options to create and continue to build from the freshman year through the senior year. Each chapter offers opportunities for active reflection so that you can get the most out of this book. Part Two provides exercises that will help your child answer "who are you? These are questions that will not only help them discover who they are but will also help prepare them for college admissions essays. Part Three offers guidance, insights, and words of wisdom taken directly from parents and students who have successfully navigated the high school years. Part Four is a collection of resources to help support you through every step.

Although the first section of the book deals with middle school as the threshold for high school success, this book is valuable for a parent who has a child in any level of high school. I will admit that my favorite time to meet with a student who is wanting to attend college is before they are a senior...ideally as a freshman to give them the big picture of what is to come. By the time they become seniors, a great deal of their story has been created. At that point, I am just trying to help them tell their story. With many of these students, I so wish I had met them years earlier to help them understand the importance of leadership, passion projects, strong academics, community service, and making sure they are doing things that are consistent with their values and who they are. Whether your student is still in middle school, is just starting high school, is just finishing high school, or somewhere in between, there are actions that you can take to help multiply their graduation options. You will be ahead of the curve instead of saying, "Why didn't someone tell me that?" or "I wish someone had told me that earlier."

Throughout this book you will also find **PARENT ALERTS**. These are highly recommended suggestions for action. Can you skim and only read the parent alerts? No. They cannot capture a summary of the roadmap, but they do emphasize key actions you can take.

Remember, this is an active process. I encourage you to write notes and do the exercises directly in the book or to find a dedicated notebook where you can keep all of your work in one place. Break out your pencil and enjoy the journey!

PART I

THE ROADMAP

CHAPTER 1

THE THRESHOLD: MIDDLE SCHOOL

Accompanied by an expletive or two, the words "take him" thundered through the office followed by a powerful fist slamming down on my desk. Sheepishly appearing at the door was the object of this fatherly demand, a wide-eyed, slightly embarrassed middle school minion. Dad quickly blurted out, "He just doesn't get it. No matter what I say, he just isn't listening." I would soon find out that this young man had been blessed with incredible intelligence, massive athletic ability, and a solid financial backing, but for some "strange" reason had fallen into the middle school morass that somehow dictates that being "like" everyone else is preferrable to being who you are. His dad was correct: his son wasn't listening to him…but he was listening to what all of his friends were professing. The son hadn't connected the dots to see that his fellow classmates had NO idea what would really help them get ahead.

A very common dilemma of the middle school mindset is this shift from relying on parents as the source of knowledge to instead turning to friends. Thus, the enigmatic, telltale, all-knowing, this-must-be-a-middle-school-student eye roll. They haven't figured out that if they want to go to college, or go to a good college, or go to a highly selective college, or get a good job, they have to be competitive. In the long run, it will be how they are DIFFERENT, not how they are the same, that will get them ahead. But in middle school, being different is scary and can get you bullied or momentarily set aside from the "in" group. They don't know how dramatically that credential to get into the "in" group changes in just a few short years. Standing out in middle school takes a strength that many students don't yet possess. Even if math is their superpower, they are likely to think, "Well, all my friends are in the regular math class, so I will just be in that class too." What they can't see is that, if they just embraced that power, they would then get to be in the advanced math classes in high school, which will create so many more options for them later.

Middle school is a great time to start stretching who they are and discovering what they truly, genuinely love to do and to start igniting their fire to help them start to discover who they are. So, where do you start? In my experience working with middle schoolers, there are 15 critical success elements that help them prepare for their high school years and start to create options for themselves as early as possible.

1. Academics Are Paramount

The most important element of a college application is your high school GPA in rigorous classes. The exception to this is talent-based colleges like Julliard and Berklee College of Music, which are evaluating talent and proficiency in a specific area. Outside of those exceptions, most U.S. college admission counselors will FIRST look at your GPA in rigorous classes as the key indicator of whether you can be successful at their college. As an example of the importance of GPA in rigorous classes, of the 13 considerations for admissions to the University of California system, easily 9 of the 13 criteria deal directly with academic achievement (https://admission.universityofcalifornia.edu/how-to-apply/applying-as-a-freshman/how-applications-are-reviewed.html). There are many other elements that they will evaluate, but you must be able to be academically sound to maintain your admission status. They do not want to admit you and then have you flunk out or become academically ineligible to participate in collegiate sports.

So, why in the world am I discussing this in the middle school section of this book? The train leaves the station starting in middle school in terms of the academic track you may be on when you start high school. The step from middle school to high school is academically steep. Trying to double jump from middle school standard track classes to honors high school classes makes that leap even higher and harder.

Math tracks are set in middle school. Most students have completed pre-algebra in the 8th grade; in a standard track, starting in high school they would then go to algebra 1 followed by geometry, algebra 2, and some math course that is a step higher than algebra 2 their senior year. That is a standard public high school model. College admission tests knowledge through algebra 2 at minimum. The ACT even stretches into a few trigonometry concepts. Some more advanced students will complete algebra 1 while in middle school and then will be able to get in two classes more advanced than algebra 2 in high school. Some middle school students will complete two years of traditional high school math while they are in middle school and then have the option of taking college-level math courses while in high school. Examples of these courses would be AP statistics, AP calculus AB, AP calculus BC, capstone classes, IB HL math classes, and linear calculus. Being able to take these levels of classes shows an interest and passion for math and the ability to do well in more advanced courses. If your middle school student tells you they want to be a doctor or still have extensive Lego models strewn about their rooms (think budding engineer), they need to try to get on an advanced or honors math track. That means nail that pre-algebra class. If your student struggles in math, get them help! Have them see their teacher before or after school or at lunchtime, put together a study group for them, or get them a peer tutor or a professional tutor. Just do it.

English is also part of the middle school academic journey. This includes both reading and writing. If they still write at a 4th-grade level with a questionable vocabulary, then now is the time to seek out extra support. My favorite eye-opener for parents is to have them get a copy of the Barron's HSPT (High School Placement Test) preparation booklet and have them give the test to their child with the listed time limits the summer between their 7th and 8th grade years. This test is the one students must take at the beginning of their second semester in 8th grade to be admitted into private Catholic high schools. I have had many students take this test and answer fewer than 50% of the questions correctly. If your student is scoring in this range or even lower, they need help, NOW. Many students will run out of time the first time they take this test, especially in reading, but not finishing is not finishing and contributes to the score. If they struggle, here are some strategies to help them:

- Sign them up for tutoring.
- Set up a vocabulary cards box that they can work on outside of school with incentives for vocabulary growth (think ice cream).

- Have them complete a set of Wordly Wise workbooks.
- Have a word of the day listed on your refrigerator and make sure they can use it in a sentence by the end of the day.
- Check their writing assignments for four-letter words like good, nice, kind, etc. and help them find replacements for these words and banish them from their writing.
- Have them read a piece of the newspaper to you. Most newspapers are written at a 6th-grade level. Any words they don't know need to go into that vocabulary box.

Words are power. Words can help get you out of trouble. The minute a child opens their mouth and starts to talk, people will start to form opinions about their academic track and abilities. Help them put their best foot forward in the world of words.

2. Learn to Love Reading

Reading is so important that it will come up time and time again throughout this book. If your student "is not a reader" (I hate those words), you need to get help fixing that while in middle school. Help them find that subject or author that makes them want to read. In middle school, I discovered reading through *Reader's Digest's* condensed classic books. Now, I don't normally recommend condensed books because you can lose some of the writing brilliance, but the concepts and internal struggles found in these books were so much more advanced and interesting to me than normal middle school books. I devoured Hugo and *Wuthering Heights* and *Emma* and *The Count of Monte Cristo* and became a lifelong reader in middle school. I still read at least 16 books every summer and always have a stack of "next books" to read by my bedside. Fiction, nonfiction, it doesn't matter.

I struggle with choosing my favorite author because I have so many. High on the list would be anything by Steinbeck, *The Sound and the Fury* by Faulkner, and *A Gentleman in Moscow* by Amor Towles. (See other reading suggestions in the Resources section.)

By the way, some college applications will ask that very question: What is your favorite book? Have you shared your favorite author with your child? Do they see you reading? Do you ever talk about what you are reading? In our family, we actually started a family book club where each parent and each child would pick a book and we would have two months to read them. Then we could talk about the books or, at the very least, have a common set of knowledge for discussion. I have been stretched to read books I wouldn't have normally read.

My favorite author is:	
…Because:	
My favorite book is:	
…Because:	
The best book I have ever read is:	
My child's favorite book is:	

Other books by that same author my child could read include:	

Create a family book club. Try it for one year with about 10 weeks to read each selection. Have each family member select a book and collectively choose an autobiography.

FAMILY MEMBER	BOOK CHOICE

PARENT ALERT: Read!

3. Musical Training

One of my big pushes for middle school students is to get them involved with music. Let them pick the instrument if you can, but "make" them try to play an instrument. Even if you don't play one yourself, help them find their voice through music. It was a family value in our house that each of our children had to play a musical instrument throughout middle school. They could change the instrument if they wanted to as they progressed, but they had to play something. One of our daughters discovered jazz music and improvisation through the saxophone. Wow, what a way to find out who you are and find your own music and voice! In addition, there is a well-known correlation between math and music abilities. We saw this firsthand through our math-gifted daughter, who went on to play four musical instruments and work at the Jet Propulsion Lab at NASA. Much of this started through the music program at the middle school, which was led by a passionate music teacher. In high school, they chose to stop music lessons, but they did not stop loving music. Each found other ways to make their hearts fly, but the study of music will always be a part of who they are. It opened doorways to many more curiosities. They have never regretted learning how to play a musical instrument, cook, swim, or take care of an animal or how to sing or dance or grow a tomato plant. All of these are prime middle school activities as they transition from children to adolescents and start to become more independent and define their own identity.

Music is an important part of many students' lives. Many listen nonstop, as evidenced by the earphones that seem to be permanently attached to their heads. If they are listening to something nonstop, you know it is affecting them. Shouldn't you know who and what are influencing them? Do you ever talk with your child about music? What do you like to listen to and why? What are your favorite songs...genres...composers...singers... groups...instruments? What are theirs?

What do you like to listen to and why?

What are your favorite songs?

Genres	
Composers	
Singers	
Groups	
Instruments	

What do they like to listen to and why?

What are their favorite songs?

Genres	
Composers	
Singers	
Groups	
Instruments	

Support your child in getting involved with music. Starting in 6th grade, ask them what musical instrument they want to learn to play, and ask them every year to make sure the interest hasn't changed. Depth is important, but you will never be able to teach them depth if you are not helping them pursue something that captures their imagination. Find them the best music teachers available. You can even look into summer programs specifically dedicated to music, such as Interlochen and Tanglewood.

What are your child's favorite song lyrics? What do the words mean to them?	
What musical instrument(s) does your child want to learn or play this year?	
6th grade	
7th grade	
8th grade	

> **PARENT ALERT:** If your child's middle school does not have a music program, advocate for one. It will be worth it for your child's growth and discovery and math scores.

4. Building Physical Confidence

Another part of middle school learning is developing confidence in physical abilities, especially at an age when they often look and act more like gangly colts than human beings. It can also give them a sense of pride in finding something that they do well. All three of our daughters explored athletics. We exposed them to a lot of options, like the musical instruments, but they got to pick the one they wanted to dive deep into. One of our daughters gravitated towards dance and went on to become a professional dancer as a Radio City Music Hall Rockette and on the national Broadway tour of *A Chorus Line*. Two of our daughters found a passion for swimming and were recruited college athletes. One went on to hold national records in distance freestyle events and to compete in the Olympic Trials while still in high school. The other was an Ivy League–recruited swimmer whose sports confidence translated into college internships at Disney, Paramount, NBC, and upon graduation landing a job as a sports writer with ESPN. She also held a second job as a swim coach in her spare time for age-group swimmers.

I worked with many high school students who had reached a high level of ability in a particular sport but due to an injury were not able to compete as varsity athletes. They found other ways to be involved with the activity they loved, including becoming referees or team managers or teaching kids or individuals with disabilities. One student I worked with became the team's statistician, a position he created for the coach. That shows resilience, which is both an essential life skill and a key characteristic colleges value.

There is power in confidence, and it is well worth the sacrifice involved with early morning trainings, after-school practices, and weekend shows and tournaments. With our daughters, as long as they loved what they were doing, we were there to support them and make sure they could always be their best. All three are tall and could easily have been targets of bullying in middle school as they stood out as "different." But they knew and believed that height was actually an advantage and an asset, not something to in any way be ashamed of or mocked for.

The teamwork aspect of their sport also was an essential part of their middle school experience. On her college application to Stanford University, where she eventually attended, my daughter was asked what her favorite word was. I was actually amazed at how quickly she wrote: "camaraderie," which means mutual trust and friendship among people with whom you spend a lot of time. She started living that word in middle school. Organized physical activities help young people to foster that try-hard attitude, understand the importance of teamwork, and learn how to handle defeat and get up again.

Each of our daughters tried many sports before they found the one that matched their interests and abilities. It had to be their sport, not one that was picked for them. So, as a parent, you must be there to help encourage them to find a sport or physical activity, such as track, and make sure that they finish the season with it and that they don't give up the minute it gets too hard. Exposing them to multiple opportunities is your job. How empowering is it to be able to say: I am a runner...a swimmer...a dancer...a football player...a soccer player...a water polo player...a basketball player...a lacrosse player...a fencer...an equestrian...a wrestler...an archer...a gymnast...a martial arts brown belt...a golfer...a black diamond skier...whatever that physical pursuit is that captures them. They are certainly not JUST that, but it can contribute to their way of thinking about what they are capable of doing or being.

> **PARENT ALERT:** Have your child try various organized physical activities to help them discover their physical talents. Sign them up and make sure they finish the season. You may discover that they are a budding Tiger Woods or Michael Phelps or that chess is their thing. Either way, they win by learning how to finish something, how to win and lose with good sportsmanship, and how to be part of a team.

5. Parent: Spelled P-A-R-E-N-T

This may be controversial, but in my experience, PARENT is spelled P-A-R-E-N-T, not F-R-I-E-N-D. There will be time to be your child's friend, but not until they have had enough life experiences to be able to talk to you as an adult...with adult reasoning and logic and a whole lot more experience. In a middle school student and even high school student, that adult reasoning and true understanding of consequences for actions is not fully developed and won't be until they are in their 20s. Again, you need to be a good listener to gain their trust, but you have the very, very, very important job of being the P-A-R-E-N-T. Don't mitigate the importance of that title by being only their friend.

Like a friend, you will see the best in them and will help them recognize those qualities. Like a friend, you will believe in them and support them. But the obligations of a parent carry so much more weight in terms of responsibility and trust and reliance. Letting a child have whatever they want whenever they want it is not going to teach them the life lessons they need to learn. It would be like giving them the fish without teaching them how to fish. It would be teaching them how to forever be a child. Being there to pick them up when they fall down is more important than never letting them fall, because in life everyone falls sometimes. Your job is different from and so much more important than just being a friend. "Parent" comes from the Latin root word *paree*, which means to bring forth. That is exactly what you are challenged to do...bring forth all the best in your child. This includes aspects of their work ethic, ability to be flexible, depth of generosity and compassion, resilience, tolerance, and sense of self. That's a pretty important job, and you are their first role model.

Remember the young man from the beginning of the chapter who was standing in front of me looking a bit like a wet kitten who had just fallen into the toilet and knew he needed to get out but didn't know how? Here is what I said to him: "Well, Matt (name changed to protect the innocent), tell me where you want to find yourself in four years and let's put together a detailed plan as to how you'll get there." His look was one of pure shock. No one had asked him that before nor had he even thought about it. His answer was a big indication that he needed to start thinking more about it. He professed slowly that he and his buddies were just going to play video games and wrestle and eat at home (lots of eating going on with middle school boys). So, at that very moment, I told Matt he needed to stop and really think about that answer again. I was going to allow him to hit the redo button and talk to his dad and mom and come back to me with a real answer to that question. Then and only then could we put together that detailed plan to get there. And yes, things happen, plans change. One injury can eliminate athletic scholarship plans. One "stupid mistake" in high school can rewrite where you end up or if you're able to go to college. But I am a firm believer in the fact that you need a plan. In fact, I believe you need Plan A and Plan B and Plan C. This young man eventually got it and ended up attending Harvard as a recruited athlete.

Let me be blunt for a moment: you are not doing your job as a parent if your child is spending multiple hours on social media or in the gaming world every day. Oh, yes, there's the argument that they are going to become a professional gamer. Well, here are the statistics on that: the probability that any new player will become a pro gamer is about .00008%, according to raiseyourskillz.com, with the average income being about $30,000 a year. Yes, as a full-time professional doing it 40 hours a week plus practice time. Help your child do the math on what that would mean to their lifestyle. Many professional gamers make only $12,000 a year. There are, of course, rare exceptions to those statistics, but they are just that: exceptions. If they like gaming, help encourage them to learn computer game coding or design. Maybe take a summer camp where they can explore those skills and talents.

A child's decision-making abilities don't completely mature until they are in their mid-20s. According to one of the leading experts on adolescence, Laurence Steinberg, PhD: "Although adolescents likely possess the necessary intellectual skills to make informed choices…they lack the social and emotional maturity to control impulses, resist peer pressure, and fully appreciate the riskiness of dangerous decisions."

Is their bedroom door closed? Do you know what they are doing if their door is closed? Can you easily see their screens? Wait, who owns that room? Who owns that computer? That cell phone? You need to help them with that skill development while they are still at home. Consider implementing a "no earplug zone" in certain areas of your home or in your car, which will help provide more opportunities to ask open-ended questions and then listen with all your heart to their answers. Too much of "a fun thing" like playing video games, binge-watching TV, eating unhealthy food, "hanging out," social media, shopping, and partying can negatively impact their motivation. Teenagers need to work hard now and make short-term sacrifices to obtain long-term future goals.

> **PARENT ALERT:** PARENT is spelled P-A-R-E-N-T, not F-R-I-E-N-D.

6. Define Your Family Mantra

Could your child tell me in a short sentence or two what your family believes in?

My mother used to always tell me: "To thine own self be true." She wanted me to believe in myself and my abilities. If you asked my children what some of our key family values are, I would hope they would tell you:

- You have to FINISH; go all in when you start something.
- Set a goal: short-term, mid-term, long-term. Make it a stretch and achievable and DO IT.
- Think BOLD and never underestimate what you can do.

If I could sum up my family mantra in a few short words, it would be:

The things I find myself saying over and over and over again to my child are:

Is this consistent with what you want your family mantra to be? If not, how can you change the dialogue to help these align?

PARENT ALERT: Declare your family mantra.

7. Keep Them Busy

One of the best ways to get kids out from behind their screens and to make sure they do not have time to develop idle hands or idle minds is to keep them busy. Support them in being engaged with faith-based activities, music, exploration, athletics, reading, being outdoors, learning a new skill, or community-based volunteering. Don't let middle school become a wasteland. You get to participate in their development here, but have some fun with it. Making lists and goals can always be a good way to start.

Reading goals. What books does your child want to read this year? Even better, let's break it down to three nonfiction and three fiction books. These should be age appropriate, of course (check out www.k-12readinglist.com), and should be related to topics your child is interested in. And you need to read them too. What, you think you are too busy? No, it is your job to not be too busy to show your child that you love to read. It's not just the teacher's job, but YOUR job as well. One of the added benefits is that it gives you something to talk about together.

	6th Grade	7th Grade	8th Grade
What three nonfiction books does your child want to read this year?			
What three fiction books does your child want to read this year?			

Explore interests and curiosities. Come up with other lists that you know appeal to your child's interests or curiosities:

- What animals have you seen in the wild, and what three additional animals do you want to try to see in the wild this year?
- What regional, state, or national parks have you been to, and what are two new ones you would like to visit this year?
- What three new skills do you want to learn how to do this year? This should be specific, tangible, measurable, and something they can reasonably achieve that will build their confidence. As just a few ideas to get you started: juggle, throw a paper airplane 50 yards, walk a tightrope, zip-line, ski, ice-skate, make a three-layer cake, swim 500 yards, crochet, learn how to take a publish-worthy photo, build a 12-foot tower out of marshmallows and toothpicks, grow an herb, fruit, or vegetable garden.

The year of the... You can also build a set of questions around "the year of the..." and explore what thing or event your child would want to learn more about over the course of the year. It could be The Year of the Submarine, The Year of Finland, The Year of the Civil War, or whatever sparks their interest that year. Maybe it has a piece of family significance or is just something they want to learn more about. Having a theme for the year that has an academic base or inspires curiosity is important. Being able to show curiosity will be one of those skills that can pay VERY BIG dividends in future years. Go beyond the surface level and really dive deep into the topic.

Investigate family history. Does your child know your family's genealogy? Have them help you research it and find out more about who they are through family history. If grandparents are still alive, encourage them to interview each grandparent about their lives and take notes with a notebook like a reporter. It may even be a good idea to record the conversation. Help them write questions ahead of time. We may sometimes forget this, but grandparents are not dinosaurs. If they are applying to college, the essence of their essay is built around the question: "Who are you?" This is a way to start that process of finding out where they came from. If your child likes arts and crafts, help them produce a frameable family tree that you can add to your home.

Helping others. Another category of self-esteem–building questions would be: Who do you want to help this year, why is it important to help them, and how will you do it? It could be an individual, a family, or a piece of the community. One idea would be participating in a walk to raise awareness and funding for a particular disease, such as Walk for Cancer or Walk for the Alzheimer's Association. You can also put together a car wash to raise money for a family that needs help or organize something through your faith-based organization. It feels good to help someone else, even when you are only 12 or 13 years old. What an empowering thing to be able to say: "This year, I helped…"

> **PARENT ALERT:** Have your child "DO STUFF" consistent with who they are.

8. Know Their Friends

Usually, a great part of social and emotional development takes place in middle school. Friends start to become more and more important. Groups start to develop. Everyone wants to be LIKE everyone else and be LIKED by everyone else. They want to keep their head down and become part of the group. They start to see parents as knowing less and less about life, so rather than turning to parents, they turn to peers. Being a part of the "in" crowd becomes a coveted position for many, and your child may start to transform into a different child before your very eyes. The dreaded Boyfriend or Girlfriend starts to appear. It becomes imperative that you know who your child's friends are. One of the best ways to do this is to listen to their banter in the back of your car when you drive them. You can even ban cell phone use while you are driving them as a group in the car. Don't let them hide. Yes, it is a part of your job as a parent.

Ask yourself these questions:

- Who are your child's three best friends?
- Do you like these friends? Why or why not?
- Do these friends help your child become a better person?

> **PARENT ALERT:** Name your child's three best friends.

9. Vanquish Vaping

Vaping has been on the rise, even for children as young as middle schoolers. Be on the lookout along with other concerned parents for signs that your child might be vaping. The CDC website (www.cdc.gov) has a number of excellent resources on the evils of vaping. Bottom line: vaping is NOT OKAY. Vaping involves nicotine and has been found to be a MAJOR gateway substance to cigarette smoking and marijuana use. Research has shown that marijuana is the main gateway drug for more lethal drug use and addiction. If you are interested in knowing what life is like as a family with a child who is addicted to drugs, I recommend reading *Beautiful Boy* by David Sheff. I had a family member who struggled with addiction, so I know firsthand how tragic it is.

Talk about vaping with your child. Let them know that it can set one on a dangerous path and can ravage and destroy their lives. Let them know vaping is not acceptable because you love them too much to let it happen to them. I have spoken with middle school and high school students who are petrified to use the bathroom at their school because it is where all the vape users go to smoke. When the entire bathrooms are filled with smoke, security goes in and writes up everyone for detention or suspension if there is evidence of vape smoke, regardless of whether that child was smoking. If they happen to find themselves in a bathroom where someone else is vaping, they are at risk of having their permanent school record blemished. Some students have told me that they limit the amount of fluid they drink during the day so they do not have to use the restroom while at school. This is a particularly dangerous thing to do in areas like the Phoenix desert. If you have any suspicion that your middle school student is involved with drugs of any sort, get them professional help right away. DO NOT WAIT! Have the hard conversation NOW. Zero tolerance.

> **PARENT ALERT:** Read *Beautiful Boy* by David Sheff and have a family conversation about vaping.

10. Set Boundaries for Social Media and Phones

Middle school may be the first time a student gets a cell phone or becomes introduced to social media. Remember, as a parent, these are all things that are under your control and financial discretion. A child can have a cell phone only if they have earned the right to have one. You have to be allowed to TRUST BUT VERIFY that the "tool" is being used appropriately, properly, and compassionately. Make sure they know what is and is not allowed. Set boundaries around when it can be used and who can be called. Put restrictions in place using settings on the device. Verify that it is being used according to the rules; if it isn't, you have the right to remove that tool until the child is able to follow your rules and expectations. Tears, shouts of you being an ogre or ogress, and refusal to talk to you are all signs of them pushing the limits to see how serious you are. And you are very serious about social media, because you are a P-A-R-E-N-T and not just a F-R-I-E-N-D. You know that certain missteps with social media can have lifelong consequences. Develop house rules for computer/social media/phone use and post these somewhere in the house where they can be easily seen on a day-to-day basis.

> **PARENT ALERT:** Create a contract for them to sign where the consequences for not following the rules are delineated and, MOST IMPORTANTLY, have them sign it.

One of my favorite social media and cell phone contracts can be found on www.verywellfamily.com. "A Social Media Contract for Tweens and Parents" and "Sample Cell Phone Contract for Parents and Teens" by Jennifer O'Donnell are reprinted below to give you an idea of what can and should be included.

Social Media Contract for Tweens

- I understand that using social media is a privilege and not a right. I understand that my privileges may be revoked by my parent(s) or guardian(s) at any time for bad behavior, uncooperative behavior, or for allowing my grades to fall, or for failure to chip in and help with family chores and responsibilities.
- I understand that I should never use social media to torment or harass a schoolmate, teacher, or any other person. I will not participate in online fights, threaten others, or encourage others to behave badly.
- I understand that my parent(s) or guardian(s) have the right to review my online behavior and that they should have access to my password and accounts.
- I understand that I will not use inappropriate language on social media or post photos that could be embarrassing to myself, my family members, friends, or classmates.
- I understand that I should keep my parent(s) or guardian(s) informed if others are using social media to bully, threaten or harass me.
- I understand that the best policy regarding social media is, "If you can't say anything nice, don't say anything at all."
- I understand that I will get my parent(s) or guardian(s) permission before establishing an account with a social media site such as Facebook, Twitter, or Instagram.
- I understand that bad behavior on social media could reflect poorly on me and my family.

Social Media Contract for Parents or Guardians

- I promise to help my child identify the pros and cons of using social media.
- I promise that I will check my child's social media accounts on occasion to be sure that he/she is staying safe and behaving appropriately on social media.
- I promise not to overreact if I see something on social media that concerns me. Rather, I will calmly discuss the matter with my tween and work through the situation together.
- I promise that my child may come to me at any time to troubleshoot a social media challenge, such as bullying, taunting, or other bad behaviors.
- I promise that should my child break our social media rules I will enforce fair but firm consequences for the behavior.
- I promise to set a good example on how to behave on social media for my child by avoiding profanity, mean-spiritedness, bullying, sarcastic, or other antisocial behaviors or attitudes.
- I promise to take immediate action if I determine that my child's safety is in any way in question due to social media, which may include confiscating my child's phone, contacting my child's school or local law enforcement officials if necessary.

Parent's Signature: _____

Date: _____

Tween's Signature: _____

Date: _____

From: Jennifer O'Donnell, "A Social Media Contract for Tweens and Parents,"
www.verywellfamily.com.

Phone Contract for Tweens

[Tween's Name] Cell Phone Responsibilities

- I will share my phone's password with my parents and they may use it to check my phone at any time.
- I will not send threatening or mean texts to others.
- I will not text or place phone calls after 9 p.m.
- I will keep my phone charged at all times.
- I will answer or respond promptly when my parents contact me.
- I will not bring my cell phone to the family dinner table.
- I will not go over our plan's monthly minutes or text message limits. If I do, I understand that I may be responsible for paying any additional charges or that I may lose my cell phone privileges.
- I understand that I am responsible for knowing where my phone is, and for keeping it in good condition.
- I will obey the rules of etiquette regarding cell phones in public places. I will make sure my phone is turned off when I am in church, restaurants, or other quiet settings.
- I will obey any rules my school has regarding cell phones, such as turning them off during class, or keeping them on vibrate while riding the school bus.
- I will alert my parents when I receive suspicious or alarming phone calls or text messages from people I don't know.
- I will also alert my parents if I am being harassed by someone via my cell phone.
- I will not use my cell phone to bully another person.
- I will send no more than _____ texts per day.
- I understand that having a cell phone can be helpful in an emergency, but I know that I must still practice good judgment and make good choices that will keep me out of trouble and out of danger.

- I will not send embarrassing photos of my family or friends to others. In addition, I will not use my phone's camera to take embarrassing photos of others.
- I will not use my phone to buy or download anything without asking permission first.

Consequences

- I understand that having a cell phone is a privilege and that if I fail to adhere to this contract, my cell phone privilege may be revoked.
- If needed, I may help pay for the cost of the phone and/or for excess charges that I incur without permission from my parents.
- I understand that my cell phone may be taken away if I talk back to my parents, fail to do my chores, or fail to keep my grades up.

Parent Responsibilities:

- I understand that I will make myself available to answer any questions my child might have about owning a cell phone and using it responsibly.
- I will support my child when they alert me to an alarming message that they have received.
- I will alert my child if our cell phone plan changes and impacts the plan's minutes.
- I will give my child _____ warning(s) before I take his or her cell phone away.

Signed: _____ [Tween]

Signed: _____ [Parents]

Date:_____

From: Jennifer O'Donnell, "A Social Media Contract for Tweens and Parents,"
www.verywellfamily.com.

Know that bullying happens both virtually and in person and can be devastating to a child. Don't be afraid to ask your child if they are being bullied or if they have a friend who is being bullied. I have worked with three students this year alone who had actually become suicidal after being bullied in middle school and early high school. Kids who are in these situations need adults to help make it stop. Be the adult in the room. Don't rely on the school to make the bullying stop, because they may not do anything.

My neighbor's daughter serves as one frightening example of bullying and how little schools do to intervene. She was in middle school and was being sexually assaulted by a young man who would grab her breasts whenever he passed her in the hallway. Although many students had observed this happen and had substantiated the young girl's cry for help, the school said they could do nothing because the young man claimed that the multiple incidents were just accidents. He said he had slipped and grabbed her to maintain his balance. The school would not take any disciplinary action. The young lady asked him multiple times to stop, and her parents called his parents to ask him to stop, but nothing happened. Because it had crossed the line to sexual assault, the parent took the young man and his family to court and obtained a restraining order. The girl was so traumatized that she went to therapy. The school "talked" to the young man but refused to give any disciplinary actions. Eventually, rather than the young man being asked to leave the school, my neighbor decided to enroll her daughter in another school where she had no further incidents. The irony is that the bully got to stay at the school and my neighbor's daughter did not.

It is your job to advocate for your child, and that requires knowing what is going on in their lives. This becomes especially challenging with technology and social media. Be aware of cyberbullying and make sure your child is not being victimized online.

11. Keep Them Healthy

Middle school is the perfect time to get your child to become a student of nutrition. It's also a great opportunity to spend some time together and learn how to cook basic things. The food pyramid is a basic and easy concept to teach. You can print out a copy of it and hang it on your refrigerator door. Let them plan a week of meals. Get them to commit to try one new food every month. Whenever the seasons change, there is usually a variety of new fruits and vegetables at the grocery store or farmer's market. Talk about your favorite types of foods from each food group.

Favorite protein(s)?	
Favorite carb(s)?	
Favorite fruit(s)?	
Favorite vegetable(s)?	
Favorite exercise(s)?	

12. Talk and Listen

Hearing what they are saying to you is very important. How you are listening is also important. Are you listening passively or actively? In other words, are you hearing what they are saying only from your perspective, or are you hearing it from theirs based on their experiences? Are you thinking about what you are going to say next, or are you directing your attention solely to what they are saying? Often, parents have to sift through their child's words and the origin of the words to determine if the words are truly theirs or something they are parroting from what they have heard from friends or media outlets. Or maybe they are just trying to get a reaction out of you.

When they are talking, you can even place your hand or finger nonchalantly up by your ear to remind yourself to listen and of the old adage that speaks to the wisdom of being given two ears and only one mouth. If you are not sure of the origin of something they are saying, ask them *why* they think that way. Who says that? Can they defend that position? Offer your opinion and even engage in a debate if they are in a listening state themselves. But, to be a good debater, you MUST be a good listener. Remember, although it is OFTEN hard to tell, they ARE listening to you.

Ever since I was a young child, I could swear like a sailor in Finnish. Growing up, my 100% Finnish father, who did not actually speak English until he started kindergarten, was a strong believer that children are always listening to you. Whenever he hurt himself at home or was upset because his Green Bay Packers were losing, he would swear in Finnish because he did not want his children picking up English swear words. "Don't swear in front of the kids," my mother would remind him. Well, the result was that I learned an expansive vocabulary of Finnish swear words. I was listening.

Being a huge Broadway fan, I have to quote from "Into The Woods Finale/Children Will Listen" by Stephen Sondheim:

> Careful the things you say
> Children will listen.
> Careful the things you do
> Children will see and learn.
> Guide them along the way, children will listen
> Children will look to you for which way to turn
> To learn what to be.
> Careful before you say, "Listen to me."
> Children will listen.

Also, don't forget to talk *with* them. Ask questions. If they are giving mostly one-word responses, it tells you they may not be listening. Don't let them hide. Get inside their heads. Talk with them, not just to them. Never underestimate the power of questions. A simple "what do you think about _____?" followed up by a series of "whys" can go a long way in starting a conversation and shows that you are interested in what they think. Plus, it's an interesting table turn from when they were two years old and would ask you incessant "whys" about everything imaginable. You can also ask very specific questions like: What was the highlight of your day? What made you laugh today? Did you make anyone laugh today? Who helped you the most today? Was there anything you didn't understand at school today?

Some of the best listening I have ever done in my life was with my eyes. Right now, go into your child's room, sit on their bed, and look around the room. See what it is that they have chosen to keep closest to them. What is the first thing that they see when they get up every morning? What screensavers are they using on their phone or computer? They are telling you important things about their lives without words.

In my child's room, I see:
What stickers, screensavers, or backgrounds do you see on their phones, computer, water bottle, notebook, or backpack?
What are the common themes? What is your child telling you with these items?
Now think about what this really means. Does it reflect what you know about them? What can you do to make sure what they are showing you matches with what they are telling you? Are you hearing the same story they are showing you?

> **PARENT ALERT:** Find time each day, whether it's during dinner or while you are in the car together, to get your child talking and to LISTEN to what they say.

13. Help Them Believe In Something Bigger Than Themselves

Being a part of something bigger than yourself helps in defeating isolation and depression and can enforce a feeling of happiness, which becomes increasingly important in middle school. Scientific research shows that having that connection to something "beyond self" makes us happier and healthier. Whether that is a spiritual or religious belief, a belief in nature, the cosmos, or humankind, or an international identity, whatever it is that your family values support needs to be explored NOW. Your child needs to be able to communicate it to others and they need to BELIEVE that there is more to being alive than just what they can see. For our family, it was a belief in God. If someone asked your child "what do you believe in?", what would your teenager say? If you don't know…ask them. If they don't know, help them find it.

I want my child to know that they belong to something that is bigger than themselves and will support that effort by:

I want my child to believe in:

> **PARENT ALERT:** What is your child's purpose in life? Help them find it. Help them declare it. Help them own it.

14. Practice Thankfulness

Gratitude is a practice parents can help their child foster, and middle school is a great time to do this. Start by helping your child make a list of people whom your child feels have assisted them recently. Once a month or every few months, have them write a thank-you letter to someone who has helped them. This could be a family member, teacher, coach, faith-based leader, tutor, friend, librarian, babysitter, sibling, bus driver, principal, counselor, doctor…the list is infinite. The key is to get them started on a path of thankfulness, which doesn't just mean being thankful; it means reaching out and showing another human being that they are appreciated. They can hand deliver the note or send it by mail, email, or text, however they want to do it. This is an activity that you need to oversee and talk with them about to ensure appropriateness. Maybe even join them by writing your own notes of thankfulness as they write theirs. The file that I have never been able to throw away from my many years at Scottsdale Education Center was my file of thank-you notes from students and parents. If you have ever been the recipient of a thank-you note, you know that warmth of knowing you have done something to help someone.

DATE	NAME	RELATION-SHIP	HOW THEY HELPED ME

> **PARENT ALERT:** Once a month or every few months, have them write a thank-you letter to someone who has helped them.

15. Be Their Champion, Advocate, and Cheerleader

Another parental job in middle school is being their NUMBER ONE FAN. You are their champion. You are their advocate. In middle school, children are still learning to find their own voice. Whenever humanly possible, you need to be there for their games, matches, performances, and events. Learn the lingo of their sport, including basic aspects of strategy. You need to be a student of what they love. You need to be able to understand their frustration when something doesn't go right. Help them see the bigger picture when they are not chosen for a spot and help them "EARN THE RIGHT" to have it the next time around. Help them understand that just doing the minimum does not a superstar make. In fact, it does not even make a good teammate. For anyone to get good at something, they have to practice. In academics, that practice is called homework. In sports, it is not just doing the workout but doing it the best that you possibly can. My husband would often ask our daughters, "Were you the hardest working swimmer/dancer in the pool/studio in the world today? If not, what would you like to work on for next session?" It was a reminder that they would get out of their workout or class exactly what they had put into it.

When a child starts high school, they are expected to have started to develop their own voice. Teachers and counselors often prefer talking with the student and NOT the parent. So, beginning to develop their own ability to stand up for themselves and voice their needs is an important skill. But know they will still need your intervention and assistance to articulate those needs for certain things during this preteen and early teen stage. It's a learning process.

Some of you may be facing the "what if I am not a natural coach?" dilemma OR the "they don't listen to a word I say" dilemma. First of all, you may not think they are listening, but at some level they do hear you and if you say it enough it does soak in. You could always ask them to repeat back to you the things that you really want them to hear, things like your family mantra, self-belief proclamations, or courage statements. There are many examples of things that you can say to your child to keep them focused and positive. If you really do struggle with knowing what to say, highlight your favorites from the list below and make sure you are saying the ones you feel are key for your child that day in the morning before they go to school. If you feel like it is something that could help them throughout the day, text them or leave them a voicemail with just that message.

In addition to the specific phrases below, there are some broader themes that can be helpful to keep in mind. First, middle schoolers struggle with believing in themselves. Having interviewed thousands of high school and middle school students, self-doubt is one of the biggest hurdles they have to overcome. Children this age often feel like they have a lack of self-belief and self-knowledge. This gets in the way of their ability to be resilient and to rebound. They need encouragement and to be reminded of who they are. Second, encouragement also includes steering them away from the things that can harm them and addressing those directly. Don't shy away from simple reminders about expectations that they won't do drugs, cheat, steal, lie, drink, bully, or have unprotected sex. Make sure they know your position and the consequences. Finally, always remember your family mantras. When in doubt, these can always be go-to phrases.

I have to say, I was lucky to be raised by a father who was a three-sport college athlete and a high school coach. He always seemed to know what to say to me to get me up and going, and I used many of those same encouragements with my own daughters. Some of these are things you might say at the end of the day or as they leave the house or car in the morning. Some could be reworked to become the family mantra. Even a few short words can be an effective way to quickly remind your child about what is important. Just know that they hear you.

Here is a list of sayings that can be helpful:

- You got this.
- I am rooting for you.
- You have lots of people in your corner…don't forget it!
- You are not alone.
- Hang in there.
- Stop doubting yourself. You can do this.
- Remember: no one else is you and that is your SUPERPOWER!
- Your power is in your uniqueness.
- Apply the best of you to that today.
- Think outside the box.
- Get back up and try again.
- "The only place success comes before work is in the dictionary." – Vince Lombardi
- Create it!
- Let's go!
- Keep fighting.
- Don't get ahead of yourself. Take it one day at a time.
- Give 110% today.
- Five stars!
- Nicely done!
- You've improved a lot.
- You're a fast learner.
- You should feel good about your progress.

- If you stumble, make it part of your dance.
- It always seems impossible until it is done.
- It is easy to give up. Let's remember why we started.
- I believe in you.
- You are a gifted _____.
- Finish long and strong.
- Think bold.
- Remember to embrace who you are.
- Character counts.
- Be smart.
- Make good choices.
- Avoid temptation.
- Drive carefully.
- Take care of yourself
- I hear you.
- I hear you, but…
- "No…because…"
- I see why you may feel that way, but have you ever considered…
- I'm sorry you feel that way…
- It is time to make a change. What we're doing isn't working. We need to shake things up to make them work.
- I'm watching. I'm listening.
- Did you see/hear today's news headlines?
- What did you do today?
- What did you learn today? Share it with me.
- I'm your biggest fan and will always be there for you.
- As a family, _____ is important to us.
- I am proud of you.
- I am proud of you for_____.

- I am proud of the way you _____.
- I love you.
- You are loved more than you could ever know.
- I love you because _____.

PARENT ALERT: You are not your child's friend, you are their CHAMPION!

Conclusion

As a middle school parent, it is your JOB to foster critical success skills in your child, including: (1) promoting a rigorous academic core, (2) instilling a love of reading, 3) promoting musical training, (4) building physical confidence, (5) being their P-A-R-E-N-T, (6) defining your family mantra, (7) keeping them busy, (8) knowing their friends, (9) vanquishing vaping, (10) setting boundaries for social media and phone use, (11) keeping them healthy, (12) talking and listening, (13) helping them believe in something bigger than themselves, (14) practicing thankfulness, and (15) becoming their champion, advocate, and cheerleader.

This is the launching point for high school. Make sure they have a solid foundation by being the parent who is watching and listening (really listening) and who is engaged in helping them know who they are and what they are capable of doing and becoming.

CHAPTER 2

THE HIGH SCHOOL ROADMAP

For your child, high school is a bit like being blindfolded and dropped into the middle of a forest they have never been in before, only to find, once they take off their blindfold, that they have no map to help guide them. Not only do they not have a map, they don't have anyone else with them who knows the way, nor do they have a compass, marked trails, or signs. They have no idea which direction to go to successfully make it through the forest. They are filled with fear, uncertainty, and doubt. If only they had gotten the big picture of the forest beforehand or had some idea of how to navigate by the stars. Once they are in the middle of that forest, it can be very difficult to get the perspective needed to get "home."

This book provides you with the big picture of high school so that you can help your child create their own roadmap through the forest. Their map needs to be one of their own creation, hand-drawn with a very specific end goal in mind. They need to find and embrace their superpowers, discover their passions, and have confidence to use their own voice. They need to know how they are special. You can help them do that.

What Motivates Them

Motivation is fundamental to creating and following the roadmap. It may certainly change from year to year or season to season or sometimes month to month, so it is worth having a conversation about it at least every semester.

What are your student's goals this semester?
Why?
What motivates them?
What can I do to help them?

If they can't articulate a motivation, help them find one. We all know that life gets very hard without motivation. Children like direction and goals, even if they won't admit to it. Help them connect the dots and develop a mature perspective. Most importantly, help prepare them for those moments when peers will be pulling them in the "wrong" direction.

One of the more alarming examples of peer misdirection I have seen took place on a well-known student forum site where students gave each other advice. One student asked what questions they should expect from their MIT interviewer. (And, by the way, if you are offered an interview by MIT or any highly selective school, it is very important to take it; almost 80% of the students MIT admits participated in interviews). The speculations by the students were rather amusing. One student thought they might get asked how many positions of pi they could recite, which was followed by a litany of responses of students saying they knew more decimal places of pi than the next person. Some cited 20-plus numbers (supposedly from memory) and others vowed to learn the answer out to 25 places for the interview. The irony is that the purpose of the interview is to get an idea of how well the applicant can communicate and can carry on a conversation, not just reiterate sequenced numbers. The students had NO IDEA what the interview was for, and yet they somehow felt qualified and compelled to offer streams of incorrect information to their peers.

Three Types of High School Parenting Styles

Over the years, I have worked with many parents and have observed several distinct patterns in how they approach helping their high school children prepare to have multiple options after graduation. All three of these approaches are common, and I will share which one, in my experience, is the most successful.

1. Grades, Grades, Grades

For these parents, GPA in rigorous classes RULES. And, unless the student is applying to talent-based programs like Julliard, that is generally true; for college admission officers, it is the best metric for determining the likelihood of academic success in college. They want you to succeed and to graduate. Grades will undoubtedly be the first element of your application that they look at. Having a strong academic profile can also help you greatly in your performance on college admissions tests. It is definitely paramount that you have a strong academic showing to have lots of college options.

The problem with this approach is that, if your child is so engaged in maintaining a strong GPA, they may not have time to do anything else. This will not play out well, especially with highly selective colleges or colleges that are doing holistic reviews of applications. If your child is having to do four to six or more hours of homework nightly to maintain a 3.5 or greater unweighted GPA, something is amiss. It leaves very little time for them to perfect other skills. It also may indicate that they are in an academic program that may be too difficult for them. They need to be able to do other things besides JUST their academics.

The rule of thumb is that, while in high school, a student in standard track classes (not honors, IB, or AP) should be studying for approximately two hours per night, five days a week to maintain an A/B average. For an IB or multiple AP class program, that number may go up to four hours a night on a regular basis and as high as six hours on rare occasions, such as weekend projects. If your child is putting in fewer than two hours a night and is maintaining a high GPA, you may want to encourage them to try out an honors or AP class or two. If they are putting in those two hours a night in standard classes and are not able to maintain at least a 3.0 GPA in core academic classes, you may want to consider getting them help from the teacher or through tutoring.

If that still is not getting the results of at least a 3.0 GPA, there may be a need for a study skills class or a change in the way they are studying. For example, if a student is a strong kinesthetic learner, just sitting the whole time they are studying may not be the best way for them to study and they may need to incorporate more tactile strategies. If they are a strong auditory learner, they may need to say the information out loud to learn. If they are a strong visual learner, they may benefit from colored index cards and an abundance of highlighters. Everyone is wired to learn a little differently. What works for you as a parent may not be the best way for your student to study. Some students do better with a study buddy (one or two, not the entire soccer team), while others need to be alone. If changing up those factors still does not render the needed results, there may be a need for a medical evaluation to make sure the child isn't facing other learning challenges.

That being said, GPA in rigorous classes is extremely important, but it needs to be balanced with other skills and interests, such as leadership, community service, athletics, performing arts, or work experience through internship, research, or shadowing. The academics-only model does not always provide the most options for students and needs to be balanced.

2. Checking All the Boxes

Some parents have read that a child must be well rounded to get into a good college. To allow their child to have the time to check all the boxes, they enroll them in standard track classes where they can consistently get excellent grades while having time to check all the other boxes. This reasoning is valid to a certain extent, but I have worked with students who have done 50 hours of community service work in 25 different organizations and can definitively tell you that approach also is not necessarily the best way to go. Yes, initially (ideally during the freshman or sophomore year) a student may want to try a few different community service organizations to find the one they really enjoy working for or the cause they feel passionately about. But, at some point, it is better to focus your hours into a definitive area. In other words, it's better to have 25 hours in one organization than 5 hours in five different ones.

The same can be said for general activities. If you are interested in studying something in the health services arena, it could be more important to volunteer at the hospital than to have a job at a local diner. Conversely, if you are telling the college that you are interested in business, it could be more important to have a job than to have volunteered at a hospital. Make sure your activities match your interests. You don't have to, and shouldn't try to, do EVERYTHING. The "check all the boxes" approach can cause unnecessary anxiety in a child. As we know as adults, there are only so many hours in a day, and therefore activities have to be prioritized. Also, especially for highly selective colleges (colleges where the acceptance rate is 20% or less), depth of interest is something they prize. Excellence in sports or performing arts or graphic arts or robotics or business that have manifested from years of practice and development is desirable. It is better to have excelled in one thing than to have dabbled in many things. Commitment, depth, and excellence are important. At colleges where there are single-digit acceptance rates, it is not unusual to see successful applicants with national and international awards for their commitment. Yes, it is important to be well rounded to the point that a student has participated in multiple domains of activities—providing community service, demonstrating leadership, playing a competitive sport or musical instrument, having a job, writing for school or local publications—but most importantly the student needs to have developed world-class skills in some area of curiosity.

3. Tightrope Walk

Put on your flexible balancing shoes because this is where the hard stuff takes place. The tightrope walk is the most successful approach because it is a healthy balance between "grades, grades, grades" and "checking all the boxes." As a parent, this balancing act between extremes is the challenge of the high school years.

I have seen students who aced 15 AP classes and 5 AP tests and graduated with a 4.8 GPA who did not get into highly selective schools. They were so consumed with their studies that they had failed to develop other skills and demonstrate commitment, depth, and excellence outside of academics. On the other hand, doing all standard track classes to have an easy academic load and to have plenty of time to "check all the boxes" also does not prepare your child for the rigors of college. Their decent GPA and robust resume may help them get into a college, but that does not mean they will be prepared for the academic requirements at the college level. Getting into college is only part of the equation; more importantly, you want them to be prepared to do well once they get there. They need to get good grades in rigorous classes, AND they also need to develop skills from experiences outside the classroom. They need to develop leadership and social skills through groups or clubs, compassion and humility through community service, excellence and commitment through jobs or passion projects, and curiosity and depth through deeper exploration of an academic subject. They need to have the academics AND the life skill development. As a parent, you need to help them balance both. Is that easy? No. Is it your job? Yes.

Creating Options

Studies have shown that, when people are asked, "What do you want most in life," the most common answer (beyond Maslow's hierarchy of needs like food, shelter, and sleep) is "happiness." So, what is happiness? When I have asked this question in seminars, people often say money, fame, and love. Those are not bad answers, but the common denominator for happiness, at least for most Americans, is *choice*. Choice is the essence of freedom. For example, what if you are "free" to go out to dinner any night of the week, but the only food that the restaurants serve is pizza? Now, I love pizza as much as anybody, but I really want the ability to choose other meals as well. When you break a law and are sent to prison, the punishment revolves around complete loss of choice. You don't get to choose your cell, your cellmate, the time you wake up or go to sleep, what or when you eat. You are denied options. Parents, too, take away options as a consequence when children fail to follow the rules or make poor decisions, whether that is taking away a cell phone or video game or limiting time on the computer or time spent with friends.

In understanding choice as the essence of freedom, I would submit to you that one of your "jobs" while your child is in high school is to help them create as many options and choices for themselves as possible during their four years. Some of the decisions that they may make are "choice limiting," while others are "choice creating." You always want to stay on the creating side of the equation. Extremely bad choices can quickly put you on the five-year-plus high school plan if you are not careful.

I know a pair of young men who were high school seniors at a local private school who had both been accepted to the University of Arizona and were recruited to play on the university's Division 1 football team. They had been good friends for many years and were at the top of the world with only a few weeks left in their high school careers. Unfortunately, one of the young men got a case of "SENIORITIS," a brutal and contagious disease that suddenly debilitates high school seniors. In some rare cases, like this one, it can be academically deadly. One of these young men reasoned that, since he already had his college acceptance, he did not have to turn in his final senior English paper. He thought they were safe because their admissions letter said they were "in." The hard work was over. So, both young men decided to not turn in their final English assignment. Unfortunately, what they failed to realize was that at this high school, as in most high schools, graduation is dependent on completing four years of English. By not turning in that final assignment, they ended up failing their senior year English class. Although the college they were admitted to would not have rescinded their admission letter based on that one grade, they were unable to graduate from high school because they were missing a passing grade in one semester of English. Not graduating from high school was something that required their college admission letter to be withdrawn. They became...*da, da, duuun*...5th YEAR SENIORS. On top of that, they lost their positions on the college football team and their athletic scholarships, because NCAA Division 1 required that students graduate from high school in four years in order to be eligible to play in college.

In my role as an independent college admissions consultant, I once worked with a very bright student who had adopted her father's mantra that all you have to do is work smarter, not harder, in life to win the gold ring. Now, I agree that you need to work smart; after all, there are only so many hours in the day. But, what I discovered during my years as an undergraduate at Stanford was that there will always be someone "smarter" than you. Even students who had graduated at the top of their class with perfect college admissions scores found there was always someone smarter. Even if you are a genius, there will always be someone who is a better or higher-scoring genius. You can only truly get ahead by combining all your smarts with a ton of hard work. Which student would you admit to your college: the student with the higher GPA in rigorous classes with a slightly lower college admission test score or the one with the lower GPA in standard track classes and the higher test score? Those two combinations tell very different stories about the students, one who is trying very hard and one who is taking the easy road. I know which one I would admit.

Your child needs to understand how their actions communicate to the world and needs to be able and willing to accept the consequences of their decisions. As an employer or a coach or a college admissions director, would you want to hire, play, or admit the person who does the bare minimum? No. Jobs, athletics, and college admissions are competitive processes. Qualities of resilience, perseverance, overcoming obstacles, hard work, leadership, community involvement, passion are what you need to be helping your child develop.

Why College?

Of course, college is not for everyone. Joining the military or attending technical school or getting a special certification are also perfectly fulfilling options for a successful future. However, there are many ways college can change the trajectory of your child's life.

Money. As the saying goes, "follow the money." College graduates, on average, have a much higher earning potential than students who do not graduate from college and only have a high school diploma. The Bureau of Labor Statistics estimates the difference to be approximately $1 million in earnings over a lifetime. Also, if you look at jobless statistics, you will find that the unemployment rate of college graduates is about half that of high school graduates.

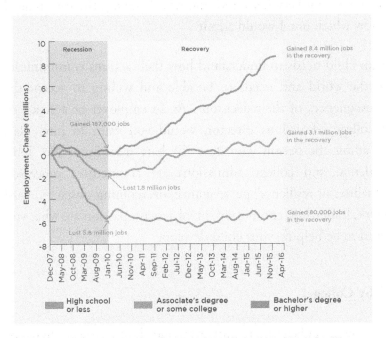

Source: Georgetown University Center on Education and the Workforce analysis of *Current Population Survey* (CPS) data, 2007-2016.
Note: Employment includes all workers age 18 and older. The monthly employment numbers are seasonally adjusted using the U.S. Census Bureau X-12 procedure and smoothed using a four-month moving average.

Lifestyle and health. With a better paying job and better health benefits, it is not surprising that college graduates are more likely to see a doctor regularly, are less likely to smoke, have a lower body mass index (BMI), and, because they tend to have higher disposable income, also tend to have healthier diets. The Brookings Institution found that an additional year of college can decrease mortality rates by 15 to 19% due in part to lower cancer and heart disease as a result of having less stress and more employment options. Moreover, a Pew Research Center study noted that 55% of college graduates report being "very satisfied" with their jobs, while only 40% of non-college graduates report that same level of satisfaction.

Expanded job options. Many job postings require a college degree just to get an interview. According to a paper posted at Georgetown.edu, since 2010 approximately 99% of jobs have gone to workers with at least some postsecondary education.

Foreign travel. College study abroad programs can be very affordable, and for some students it may be the first time they have an opportunity to go to a foreign country. International travel is an amazing way to broaden horizons and gain a better perspective on not only the U.S.'s but also an individual's place in the world.

Living away from home. Can that child cook for themselves? Balance their own checking account? Create and stick to a budget? Handle the responsibilities of a credit card? Fill up their own gas tank? Maneuver basic mass transit systems? Impose their own curfews? Balance the hours in their day? Living away from home forces young people to develop many of these skills. Unless you want your child living in your basement for the rest of their lives, they need to build these skills at some point in time.

Exposure to opportunities. I have worked with MANY high school students who are in advanced math classes and love physics but have NO idea what engineering is. There was no engineering class at their high school, so they were never exposed to an industry or major or area of pursuit that they may actually be very good at and really enjoy. Even the ones I talk to who have heard of engineering have a very limited view of what is possible. When asked if they are interested in mechanical or civil engineering, chemical or industrial, computer or electrical, biomedical or genetic, they have NO idea. While they are still

71

in high school, there are often community college classes that a high school student can attend to learn more about certain areas. Postsecondary education can expose a child to so many more classes and job opportunities than high school.

Independent thinking. One of the other key, yet sometimes intangible, benefits of college is the shift in learning emphasis to independent thought. College students are taught to question many different viewpoints and to come up with their own perspectives, not just accept someone else's. Developing their own individual viewpoint is a good skill to have when making life decisions.

New skill acquisition and the BUFFER zone. Making it through college is hard. You have to learn skills related to time management, prioritizing tasks, organization, thorough research, and general adulting. It is also a time to truly learn the consequences of actions or inactions. What happens if you forget to go to that doctor appointment? Or to take your daily medicines? Or to pay your phone bill? In fact, college can act as a bit of a buffering bridge between the ages of 18 and 22 while your child is still maturing emotionally, socially, and cognitively. Generally, parents are helping with financial issues while their child is learning some of these new skills.

Connections. Strong alumni associations can be a big boost when a young person starts to look for employment and beyond. I know that, personally, I would be more likely to hire a student from my alma mater than from another college, if the qualifications are equal. Those connections are also helpful as a basic network of people who may be able to help you in a number of scenarios, including landing internships. "Who" you know is important.

Although the long-term financial benefit of going to college is the one most people think of, there are many other reasons to go to college. Yes, you have to balance it with the debt and loans, but I always recommend that every student should create a college option for themselves. By the way, you might be surprised by how much grant money and scholarship dollars are potentially available for your student. Please do not immediately write off college for financial reasons and take some time to learn more about funding opportunities.

> **PARENT ALERT:** Talk with your child and ask them, "What do you want to be able to do when you graduate from high school?" Listen carefully to their answer. If they say they don't know, then you need to spring into action! Make sure they understand some of their options as they relate to your family values. Write down their answers here. It is a good question to revisit every semester.

What do you want to be able to do when you graduate high school?

And, by the way, not graduating from high school is <u>not an option</u>. In 2019, the high school graduation rate was 84.6%. YOU—not high school teachers, counselors, or administrators—have the best ability to keep your child in school. The Bureau of Labor Statistics has chronicled that the unemployment rate for students who go searching for a job without a high school degree is about a third higher than those who do have a high school diploma. High school dropouts earn approximately $1 million less in their lifetime than those with a high school diploma. Not completing high school means you have a much higher chance of ending up on welfare and increased odds of going to prison. Approximately 83% of prisoners in the U.S. did not finish high school.

The number one reason students end up dropping out of high school is chronic absenteeism. You have to go to school to be able to understand the material, turn in the homework and papers, pass the tests, and demonstrate mastery of the subjects required to graduate. Under COVID provisions, going to school may mean signing in virtually and showing that you have been online for a certain amount of time, have attended designated sessions, and have participated in discussions. It may mean you have completed a required number of check-ins and work. After you have missed a certain number of days each semester, your school district can withhold funding for you. The amount of money schools receive is directly tied to student attendance; if you are missing school even periodically, they become much less interested in even having you there. Special arrangements can certainly be made for chronic illness situations, but a string of unexcused absences can be a death knell for completion.

If your student is not able to complete a traditional high school model, then as a parent it is your job to make sure that they find an alternative way to earn their diploma, whether that is doing courses online or taking the GED high school equivalent test. GED tests can be used for college admission at approximately 90% of all colleges, but it will depend on the score as to whether or not a student can be admitted purely by their GED. If you yourself do not have a high school diploma and are not sure how to help your child get one, then it is even more imperative that you find an advocate team who can support you. Simply Google GED resources and you will find a plethora of options in your area. Typically, local community colleges provide low-cost GED training and coaching.

15 High School Critical Success Factors

So, how do you successfully create future options for your child while they are in high school? Over the years of working with thousands of families, I observed 15 critical factors that were common to every student success. Help your child embrace and develop these success factors so they can start drawing their own roadmap to navigate their way through the high school forest.

1. DO STUFF!!!!!

This is in all caps with lots of exclamation points for a reason. They must be action-oriented to create options for themselves. How are they ever going to find out what their passion in life is or what their superpower is without trying different things to find them? Get them outside their comfort zone on occasion. Have them commit to learning how to do three new things every semester and summer until they find what they love. Here are some activities to consider:

- Try a new physical activity, such as archery, swimming, or horseback riding
- Learn a new skill, such as cooking, sewing, computer coding, or playing a musical instrument
- Grow a vegetable garden or learn a new craft, such as pottery or woodworking
- Volunteer at a museum, zoo, animal shelter, veteran's organization, nonprofit, or hospital
- Find unique experiences in your area, such as archaeological dig sites
- Discover outdoor activities, such as hiking, camping, fishing, and visiting state and national parks
- Study a foreign language, maybe one that will be useful in daily life or one that fits with your family's lineage or background
- Master chess, sudoku, or the Rubik's cube
- Take a CPR and first aid class
- Build an art portfolio, whether that is painting, sketching, or photography
- Take a class in a subject that interests you at a community college (e.g., marine biology, astronomy, geology, cultural studies)

PARENT ALERT: ACTIVELY start finding that thing in life that interests your child. It may not be the first thing that they try to do, but pursue it to some level of proficiency beyond the first moment it starts to get hard. Provide an intellectual vitality and curiosity outside the classroom. They need to become a contributing part of the world around them. Once they know what makes their heart fly, dive deep and help them become WORLD CLASS at it. Bottom line: help them to put down their phone, get out from behind their screens, and DO STUFF!!!!!

2. Be a Reader

I am truly saddened when I meet with students who tell me with great righteousness that they "don't read," not only because I know what it means for their academic future but also because I know they are limiting their life journeys. When I was 13 years old, I sat with Quasimodo in the bell tower of the Notre Dame Cathedral in Paris through the pages of *The Hunchback of Notre Dame*. I vowed that someday I would find a way to touch those same walls that he and I had climbed together. Coming from a lower-middle class family, I didn't know if that would ever really happen, but a love of reading helped propel my achievements and adventures. Having had the children's book *Eloise* read to me when I was very young, I knew someday I would find a way to run down the halls of The Plaza Hotel in New York City while holding her hand. As an adult, I've visited the Notre Dame Cathedral and The Plaza Hotel, and my desire to do these things was sparked by those books. I have traveled down the Amazon River with Teddy Roosevelt, crashed through the steaming jungles of India, worked in the slums of pre-revolutionary Russia, walked on Mars, seen the world through the eyes of a dog, attempted to survive the horrors of a World War II concentration camp, and used lidar to discover ancient civilizations in Honduras, all because of books.

PARENT ALERT: Give the gift of reading…and thus curiosity…to your child.

One of the very best habits your child can develop as a consistent habit to help better their GPA and future options is to BE A READER. (Yes, all caps again). If your child is not a reader, it will show up on their ACT and SAT test scores. I have reviewed thousands of SAT and ACT diagnostic tests with students and without exception I can tell whether a student is a reader or not based on their reading test score. Of all the test scores, the reading score is the hardest to turn around in a short period of time. The ability to understand nuance, the implied, the inferred, and the overall speed of reading is developed over time. You can practice strategies for the reading sections of these admissions tests, but your reading comprehension actually impacts all sections of these tests.

Students need to find the subject matter, author, and genre of books that they enjoy and read more of that same type. You can start a book club with your family, with each family member picking a book every two months to read and discuss. You can also have your student:

- Write down the name of the last book they enjoyed
- Follow the book clubs of someone they admire
- Read nonfiction books about their areas of passion
- Read autobiographies about people who have accomplished great things in the same areas they hope to pursue in life
- Read a book that looks interesting from an annual list of award-winning books (check out the Resources section for a few website suggestions)
- Find a movie coming out that they want to see and make sure they read the book before they see the movie
- Ask their favorite teacher about their favorite book
- Start a book club at their school

Also, do you know what books your child is reading this year in their English class? Are they tasked with reading more than three books in the year? Have you read the books they are reading? Could you be reading the book alongside them?

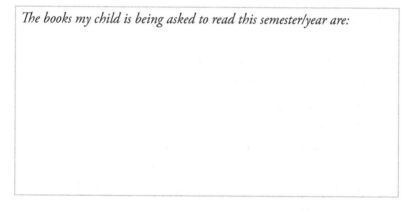

The books my child is being asked to read this semester/year are:

Having worked with such a wide variety of high schools over the years, I can tell you that there is a BIG difference in the quantity and quality of books required to be read by students when comparing standard track high school English classes, honors classes, dual enrollment classes, AP classes, IB classes, private schools, charter schools, public schools, and Catholic schools. I know of one high school standard English class that was requiring juniors to read *Animal Farm*. Back in the day, that was a book we read in middle school. And to top it off, the book was being read out loud in the class by the teacher. How will these students be prepared to read multiple high-level texts and be able to analyze, highlight, and underline them on their own in just a few years if they can't be expected to do the reading themselves as juniors?

Look at the reading lists of private high schools or high-end charter schools like BASIS or Great Hearts Classical Education and compare them to what your child is being asked to read. Now assess: Can your child be competitive when they are not being asked to stretch themselves? If the school isn't requiring it, why aren't you? An example of the top AP literature class books includes:

Invisible Man by Ralph Ellison
Great Expectations by Charles Dickens
Wuthering Heights by Emily Bronte
Heart of Darkness by Joseph Conrad
King Lear by William Shakespeare
Crime and Punishment by Fyodor Dostoevsky
A Portrait of the Artist as a Young Man by James Joyce
Jane Eyre by Charlotte Bronte
The Adventures of Huckleberry Finn by Mark Twain
Moby Dick by Herman Melville

As a sanity check, the average number of books that a successful high schooler should have read is between 25 and 30. Obviously more than 30 is great. Some of it depends on the length of the book and level of discussion that the teacher will engage in with the students. That would include summer reading assignments. If your child's English class doesn't have a summer reading assignment, that doesn't mean that you can't have a rolling summer discussion on a book or two that you are reading with your child. Avid readers may be reading a book each week during the summer. Shakespeare is a must at some point in time during high school. Many will start with *Hamlet* or *Romeo and Juliet*. To enhance a student's comprehension of the book, listening to an audio version of the book being read by a Royal Shakespearean actor or performed live can also help with comprehension. Most teachers will post their reading list for the year online at the beginning of each semester.

Books I want my child to have read by the time they graduate:
Books they want to have read by the time they graduate:

It is important for your student to develop intense vocabulary skills. Begin by having them read your local newspaper. If they feel that this level of writing is over their head, they have some work to do because most newspapers are written at a 6th-grade level. Reading news serves another useful purpose: understanding the world around them. One question I often ask students who are applying for jobs at our center is: "Tell me about the most important thing going on in the world today." That is also a question I have seen asked by selective colleges in interviews. Your vocabulary is how you communicate with the world. Don't limit your student's ability to tell their story, share their perspective, communicate their needs when looking for help, or engage with the world around them.

There are a few reading resources I recommend, including Quizlet and Wordly Wise. You may want to start with the High School Placement Test vocabulary list that is preloaded into Quizlet. There are some challenging words on that list and ones that are assumed one will know entering high school. The Wordly Wise program is often used in middle school and teaches basic root word, suffix, and pretext rules that can help you decode words you may not immediately know. In the old days, the SAT test required that you have a vast vocabulary, and you were tested on a very long list of definitions. Now they use words in context. The words you are tested on may be relatively simple but have multiple meanings. They are testing you on whether you understand the nuance of difference between each definition in the context of the line in which the word is used. In high school, your student needs to be using words that are more communicative than nice, good, really, fine, a lot, or happy.

For many college applications, college admission tests, and scholarships, your student will have to write an essay. Yes, they have to write about themselves, their beliefs, and their character. When they are asked to communicate "who are you" in 650 words or less for their Common Application essay, they can't waste any of their word count on vague words like "a lot." One of the easiest ways to build their vocabulary is through reading and figuring out the definitions of unfamiliar words through context clues or by looking it up. Beyond just being smart, your child has to be able to communicate that they are smart and their vocabulary is certainly one of the ways they do that.

While working with one student on her college application, we came to the question: "What one word best describes you?" She thought for a minute and then whipped out the word "ebullient." I laughed because it was absolutely the perfect word to describe her. She was like hummingbird wings constantly beating... an overflowing glass of champagne...an effortless nuclear-like energy. She was a reader.

3. Be Engaged

PARENT ALERT: Encourage your student to join a community service activity that interests them.

Young people need to be engaged with their communities. There are a variety of ways to go about this, and it just depends on their interests and the causes they care about. I have worked with many students who were successful in their college application process, at least partly because they demonstrated deep engagement.

I worked with one young man who was interested in becoming a doctor and studying biology in college. He led multiple walks for an Alzheimer's organization, a cause that was of particular interest to him because his grandmother suffered from the disease. He recruited his friends from school to help raise money for the organization; throughout his four years of high school, he raised over $7,000. He also formed a club at his school that would provide volunteers for memory care units. Volunteers would listen to, read to, or support the needs of the patients. During the holidays, they played musical instruments for the unit. He also arranged for educational speakers to attend the school club and talk about the latest disease prevention and detection research. Not only did he learn a lot about Alzheimer's through the process of giving back to his community, he also demonstrated to his prospective colleges that he was truly interested in medicine, had an action orientation, was a leader, and was compassionate and caring. And the keyword in that sentence is that he *demonstrated* those qualities; he did something to meet a need in his community.

Another young lady I worked with was interested in majoring in psychology and took a very big step to become a part of the local teenage suicide hotline for her community. She cared about the cause because a student at her school had committed suicide, and it deeply affected the student body. The training hours were long (over 75 hours) AND she had to make a major commitment to take calls during the month (approximately 20 hours), but she knew she was making a difference in her hometown. She also started a support group at her high school (Forever Friends) for phone support and referrals to the teen help line. She identified a need and took action to make the situation better.

Another young man I worked with was very interested in environmental science and was appalled that his school did not actively recycle. Not only did he start a recycling project for his school, but he also approached the superintendent of his unified school district and began recycling efforts at other high schools as well. At his own school, he also started a composting project. As founder of the recycling club at his school, he brought in speakers for a variety of reusable energy sources. He developed TED Talk–like clips and helped underclassmen develop their own TED Talks on reusable energy sources. His interests going forward were global, but he made a definitive impact on his local community.

Don't underestimate the impact your child can have on their community while they are still in high school. Don't let them underestimate themselves.

4. Study

Studying is an integral part of your student's job in high school. One of the biggest barometers of how successfully they are mastering the concepts being presented to them is their grade point average (GPA). For college admission purposes, GPA is paramount (the exception to that rule is in talent-based schools like Julliard where one's audition may determine admissions). This is an area that we briefly touched on earlier and will delve into much more in a later chapter, but there are a few main points to keep in mind about studying. The average amount of time a middle schooler spends on homework each night is one hour and the average for high school students to maintain a 3.5 GPA average in STANDARD track classes is two hours a day, five days a week. If your student is in any sort of advanced classes—honors, dual enrollment, pre-IB, IB, AP, capstone—that number goes up dramatically. At BASIS High School in Scottsdale, one of the top charter schools in the nation, students who are taking four to five AP classes in their sophomore year of high school often spend four-plus hours a night studying. This concept is often difficult to comprehend for really smart students who were able to breeze through middle school with minimal studying.

Things change in high school, however. The level of difficulty of the classes goes up dramatically each year and often builds on knowledge from the year before. You go from basic rote memorization in middle school to comparative analysis in standard high school classes to development of original thought for AP, IB, and dual enrollment–level classes. Things get harder, and your student will need to work harder and longer to get the same results they may have gotten in middle school. In college, they could easily spend four to six hours a night studying. In college, students are expected to do significantly more independent learning, reading, and analysis.

To illustrate what your student's college future may bring, let me tell you about the hardest class I ever took in college. International Economics was a trimester-long class that had a reading assignment of four textbook-like books. The class met twice a week for a 1.5-hour lecture on the assigned reading. The professor's lectures assumed you had done the assigned reading and built on those concepts. There was no homework for the class. No papers or projects due. No extra credit available. No quizzes or tests or midterms…except for a final. The final consisted of one question, and you were expected to sit and write for three hours in one sitting. There were no comprehension checkpoints whatsoever until the final. You were expected to have learned independently. While in high school, students learn to relish the fact that they have checkpoints for knowledge through homework and tests and quizzes and papers and projects. If they are not understanding something, they have an opportunity to remedy that issue. Don't ever miss an opportunity for a comprehension checkup. In college, they are trying to develop a student's ability to come up with original thought, not just memorization of someone else's thoughts.

Think of studying like PRACTICE. Athletes, musicians, thespians, chess players all understand the concept of practice. What would your child's sports coach do if they missed practice for a week and then said they would be ready to start at the upcoming game that weekend? Or told their music director that they would have to miss two weeks of practice because they don't have time but would still be all set for their solo? Or tried to put on a play without having rehearsals? They would be laughed at, benched, kicked out, or all of the above. Practice is the thing that helps your student get better, stronger, faster, and more agile. It helps them develop strategy and knowledge and become a truly valuable part of a team. Practice is a necessary element to get better at something. Well, the same is true for school. To get good at math, one has to DO math. That means doing homework, all of it to a high level of proficiency.

Know that college admissions directors from all over the country will tell you that the number one indicator of success in college is success in rigorous classes in high school. High school GPA isn't the only thing that college admissions look at, but in many cases it will be the first thing that they look at on the college application. They need to know a student can be successful at their school. They don't want to admit someone who has spent the past three to four years demonstrating that they don't care about school, aren't invested in learning, and have not practiced or worked hard at their academics. College coaches also want to make sure that your child will be able to remain academically eligible while they are playing for them. If they have to sit on the bench because of less-than-acceptable grades, their value to that coach and to that team diminishes. Even if your child is not planning on going to college, employers will want to know how hard of a worker they are before hiring them, and their GPA is a strong indication of their work ethic. If your child is thinking of going into the military, their performance on the ASVAB (Armed Services Vocational Aptitude Battery) is correlated with their core curriculum knowledge gained in high school.

High school GPA starts the very first day of high school. If your student doesn't do well in algebra 1, algebra 2 is going to be even more difficult. Write off the first semester of chemistry, and your student will find the second semester even tougher. I have heard many students lament that they are going into journalism, so why do they need to know biology or physics? Those classes are not just teaching concepts of science, but they are helping one develop a way of thinking and learning. They expand your ability to memorize and control complex concepts that can be applied to many things in any future profession. As a journalist, you should be working with facts and figures to support your observations and reporting of events. You have to be able to use that scientific deduction process and apply it to your writings to be credible. You not only need to know how to write, but you need to know history, science, and statistics. And above all, as a journalist, you need to be curious about the world around you.

It's time your child learned how to take notes. Note-taking is not just an important skill in school but also in life. The more a person writes down what they need to remember or information they need to comprehend, the more they will remember. I repeat: the more a person writes down what they need to remember or information they need to comprehend, the more they will. Taking notes will improve comprehension, which will lead to greater success in class. Some applications like Quizlet are helpful, but there is no substitute for taking notes in your own handwriting and with your own thoughts. Successful note-taking requires reading the material, not skimming it.

Many students think taking notes in class is simply a matter of writing down what a teacher, fellow student, or guest speaker says during an oral presentation. However, taking notes in class is more involved than this. You need to be able to determine what is important. You need to be doing something with the notes the night or afternoon after they were written. Rewrite them or commit them to memory. You need to help them develop their own shorthand so they can keep up with their teacher. Your child needs to, at the very least, be reading them regularly and getting clarification on things that don't make sense upon review.

PARENT ALERT: At the beginning of high school, take a moment to read what your child has actually written in their notes. In high school, teachers assume they know how to take notes and are not telling them what to write down like the teachers in middle school may have done. Another way to check your child's note-taking ability is to ask them to read their notes from their chemistry or history class to you that day as you drive home from school.

5. Plan

A planner is the tool to help your student create and execute their high school plan. Every adult I know has a planner. It may be on their phone or computer, on top of their desk, in a purse or pocket, or on a wall at home, but they have one. Not having a planner can be quite costly for an adult. For example, if you make an appointment with your dentist six months out, forget to write it down, and consequently forget to show up, you will be charged for that appointment anyway. The same is true for high school students, but the cost may be in GPA points. The project that is due three weeks out may be difficult to remember if you haven't written it down. Sure, the teacher posts assignments on the school website so all you have to do is check online to see what is due. But do they always keep it updated?

More importantly, your school website is not your personal schedule. If you have a big meet, game, theatrical production, or musical presentation the weekend before that big assignment, test, or project, that won't be on the website. Your student needs to take responsibility for their own schedule and not be dependent on their teacher updating things for them. That project may be due on Monday, but if you have a full weekend, you will need to get it done by Thursday night. You, the parent, need to have a planner too. One little slip can be the difference between an A and a B. Often, I have spoken to students who tell me that they have a planner, but when asked if they use it, they will say no or just sometimes. My favorite is when they tell me they use their planner "all the time," but when we check their grades, we find multiple missing assignments. That tells me they are, in fact, not using their planners "all the time," because if they were then they wouldn't have any missing assignments. Just using a planner sometimes is the same has having a refrigerator but only sometimes having electricity. A planner needs to be used like an extension of the brain. Don't let your child take up brain space trying to memorize what pages in their math book are due the next day for homework and whether it is the odd or even questions. Enable that brain space to memorize volume equations or historical facts. Your child's brain only has so much capacity, so help them be smart about how they use it.

Another effective way for them to use that planner is, instead of just writing "science test" on Friday, count back five days from Friday and write "study for science test" on every day leading up to that Friday. Your brain does much better if it has five days to work at remembering something rather than just the 24-hour cram. It also helps keep your student ready for that pop quiz.

Many students keep track of their own "academic" plan but tend to let their parents keep track of their out-of-school activity plan. These need to be on the same planner, however. While parents need to keep track of things outside of school for they are often the driver or have to coordinate multiple children's schedules, your student needs to have their out-of-school activity information as well on their academic planner. Also, be careful about having multiple planners, as you will find yourself taking more time trying to keep all planners up to date and are more likely to miss things or make mistakes.

> **PARENT ALERT:** Make sure your child has a planner and that you are checking it at least weekly until you are confident they know how to use the tool. Think of yourself as their academic coach. Everyone can use someone else's help to keep us on task and following the plan. If they don't have a planner, FIX IT NOW!!!!!!!

6. Create Goals

Where is your student hoping to end up after high school? Ivy League? Military academy? Private or public college? Out-of-state or in-state school? Community college? Technical school? Immediate employment? Gap year? Hopefully, they will have multiple options after four years of high school, but they need to have broken down the intermediate goals to get there.

Let's say the goal is to go to an out-of-state college. Your student needs to go to that college's website and see what the average or range of high school GPAs is for the students who were admitted to that school the previous year. Schools will usually publish the

25th to 75th percentile of SAT and ACT scores from their most current freshman class. Your student needs to check the college's out-of-state admission rate, because often public schools have a higher standard for admissions and a lower admission rate for out-of-state applicants. For example, University of Texas Austin's website says that, by state law, they can only admit a small number of out-of-state students. If they want to go to a college with a low admission rate, they need to make certain that their GPA and test score statistics are in the higher end of the school's admitted student ranges to be competitive. Once they have determined what those numbers should be, your student needs to write them down in a place where they can see them every day. Those become the academic goals. Don't become hyper focused on just one school, but have those stretch numbers for schools that are hardest to get into. Stretch them, think bold, and aim high. If they can't quite make those stretch GPA goals in rigorous classes, they will still potentially have other options.

I have often been asked about the idea of just taking easier or standard track classes, getting As in them, and thus preserving a very high GPA in order to bolster admission prospects. One of the problems with that plan is that scores on the college admissions tests and core curriculum knowledge often correlate. So, you may be preserving a higher GPA but it may be at the risk of lower test performance. College admissions directors know this "trick" and would rather see a student stretch themselves and get a B in a rigorous class than an A in a standard track class. In my opinion, if you cannot maintain a 3.2 GPA in honors or advanced classes, then you should absolutely be dropping down to standard track classes. But, you should definitely be taking honors classes or above in academic areas that you hope to be pursuing in college. For example, if you are planning on taking engineering in college, you should probably be taking a regular track and advanced physics class in high school if they are offered. If interested in the medical field, think of advanced classes in biology, chemistry, and human anatomy and physiology. If you are interested in business, perhaps advanced economics is on the list. If art is your interest, then your courses could include a progressive four-year participation in art classes, including AP art.

Goals can also include non-academic goals. I worked with one young lady who wanted to be a veterinarian. She started by volunteering at the local zoo. She told me her goal was to be allowed to sit in on a large animal surgery in her fourth year. We wrote that down. Her first year, she had menial jobs at the zoo, including cleaning animal pens. Whenever it got too hard or she thought she was going to quit, she told me she looked at her goal and soldiered on. Sure enough, during her senior year, she was allowed to assist with a dental surgery on a white tiger. She got to scrub in, wear the gloves, and hand over instruments to the surgeon. She was in heaven. She said the fact she had written down that goal helped her persevere.

I've worked with many Eagle Scouts, which college admissions directors love because they demonstrate a long-term, deep interest in something they are passionate about. I have seen other students focus on volunteering to a level that would allow them to be qualified for the gold President's Volunteer Service Award, work towards a black belt in martial arts, obtain a specific level of certification as a PADI-certified scuba diver, master a challenging piece of music, or raise a specific amount of money for a charity. One young lady who was interested in studying nursing in college got her certified nursing assistants certification while she was still in high school and volunteered with a hospice organization.

And when I say think BOLD...I mean BOLD. Do you want to see your art hanging in the halls of the Metropolitan Museum of Art? Create a video gaming company? Become a chef at a three-star Michelin restaurant? Stand on an Olympic podium? Touch moon soil? Cure cancer? Win a Nobel Prize in literature? Touch the walls of the Taj Mahal? Go to the deepest depths of Earth's oceans?

Research your student's goals and find out how other people got there. Your student needs to write down both in-school and out-of-school goals and keep them posted in a place they can see them on a daily basis. They should think about sharing them with their parents or grandparents or other members of their support team. Our middle daughter used to take dry-erase markers and write her goals on her bathroom mirror so she could see them every day. She went on to gain admissions to Stanford, break national swimming records, and place well at the Olympic Trials, all during her high school years. Visual goal setting works!

> **PARENT ALERT:** Encourage your child to develop a goal list with short-term, medium-term, and long-term goals, and declare it! Their success plan can't start without it.

7. Be Passionate

Demonstrating a passion markedly improves your worth to anyone you meet and can apply to all aspects of life, whether applying for college or a job, trying out for a sports team, or volunteering. A passion is the last thing you think about before you go to bed at night, the first thing you think about when you get up in the morning, and the thing that wakes you up halfway in between. It is something that you just can't learn enough about or do enough of. It is something that you know all the history about and great players in and it is that thing whose future you want to be a part of. If your passion was Irish fling dancing, you would be studying Gaelic in your spare time and would have a Celtic knot bumper sticker on your car. If you had to wear a kilt to school because there was a competition after school, you would. And, if someone stopped to make fun of you in the hallway at school because you were wearing a kilt, you would put your books down and teach them how to do the Highland fling.

A passion is something that is just a part of you, and you are willing and able to proclaim it. You may teach it or coach it or spend over 20 hours a week engrossed in it. You create in it. You referee it. You run experiments over and over in your mind trying to solve it. You spend summers doing things that involve it. You practice it over and over without complaint. You try to get better at it and work harder at it than anyone else in the world every day. A passion can be something that you are dedicated to becoming your best in to the point of being a "superpower."

First, your child needs to find their passion. That is why initially they need to try and DO lots of different things to figure out what their passion is. Then they can immerse themselves in it. Depth of study can be good, especially if it is consistent and makes sense with what they are telling others they are interested in pursuing, whether that is college, technical school, military, or wherever it is they hope to go to next. They want to develop a consistent thread or story that can be pulled through their high school story and tie it to the next endeavor.

My child believes their superpower is:

I believe their superpower is:

PARENT ALERT: A superpower is something that you do, and are recognized for doing, with excellence. Identify your child's superpower and become their champion advocate.

8. Find Self-Confidence

Help your child embrace who they are. EVERYONE HAS A SUPERPOWER. Your child needs to find out what theirs is. Everyone has excellence in them. Believing you can do something is paramount in being able to accomplish it. To have self-belief, you need to know what your inner-self is and to be okay with it. One of my favorite demonstrations of that self-belief can be found in the football stands at Stanford. When TV stations scan the crowds at the games, it is not unusual to see bands of Stanford coeds wearing big plastic lensless glasses with tape over the nose. It is perhaps the universal sign of someone being a "nerd." These glasses are a symbol of Stanford's "Nerd Nation." All students who get admitted into Stanford know they are nerds. They may have been made fun of while they were in high school because of their academic prowess, but it was one of the things that differentiated them and helped them get into Stanford. They are smart, and the glasses are a proclamation of being okay with that. They read; they write; they labor; they go deep; they DO stuff. And they are totally confident in who they are.

Is your student comfortable with who they are? Does their best friend know that what they really want to do is to go digging in the hills of Utah to find dinosaur bones? Do you know? Can you see their art hanging in the halls at the Met? Can they? They need to believe that they can do something before anyone else can. You, as their parent, need to believe it too.

With self-belief comes a certain amount of pressure and stress. As famed tennis player Billie Jean King once said, "Pressure is a privilege." Stop and think about that for a minute. The pressure your child is feeling is because someone believes in them. They may believe in themselves. You may believe in them. Their coach, teacher, music instructor, art teacher, or play director may believe in them. Their job is just to be the best they can be. That does not mean they have to be perfect, but it does mean with certainty that they have to do everything they can do to be the best they can be.

> **PARENT ALERT:** Passion can lead to superpower, which leads to goal achievement. Now that your child's superpower is identified, challenge them to embrace the privilege of pressure and to put in the work to reach their goals. If your child has been diagnosed with a learning disability or is struggling with ADD/ADHD, get them help right away as it can impact their self-confidence. There are coping skills that can help turn ADHD into a superpower.

9. Utilize Resources

Who is on your child's team? Successfully getting through high school is a team effort. In the words of 17th-century English poet John Donne, "No man is an island, entire of itself; every man is a piece of the continent." Everyone needs help to get through high school. Your child has plenty of people resources available to them, but they have to know where to look and make sure they are seeing those resources in the right light. This starts at home. Parents and extended family can be excellent resources. Does your child know your high school story? Where did you go to high school or college? What was your journey through the high school forest like? You have been through this before and have a perspective on your experience. Share that experience with your child. Other people who can help include:

Teachers	Counselors
Tutors	College and career center coordinators
Assistant principals	Principals
Coaches	Registrars
Nurses	Doctors
Respected upper-class students	Older siblings
Religious leaders	Community service organizers

PARENT ALERT: Identify at least five people who are on your student's team and have your student write down their names (not just their titles).

This next statement is one that your student needs to memorize: "Asking for help is not a sign of weakness. It is a sign of maturity." For some reason, it is an especially difficult concept for the young men I have worked with to embrace, but it is true for all of us. Tell your student to not be afraid to use their resources. Find their mentors. Collaborate with them. Let them help. Contact them regularly if needed. Let their resources help them find and stay on the trail.

MY RESOURCE TEAM	
Name:	*Title:*
Name:	*Title:*
Name:	*Title:*
Name:	*Title:*
Name:	*Title:*

10. Be Surrounded by Quality People

What is a "quality" person? Think of a quality person as someone who can help make you better. This can be a very difficult judgement to make, and it can be especially difficult to cut ties with friends who start to go in a different direction. My husband had a best friend in middle school, Jimmy, who was exceedingly smart, got all A's, quarterbacked the football team, and played drums in a band. Unfortunately, Jimmy was led to drugs by a few of his band friends. Not just any drug but LSD. My husband knew the band group well but was smart enough to avoid the temptation. All of a sudden, Jimmy stopped going to school, wouldn't answer the phone, and basically disappeared. My husband found out later that Jimmy had a bad trip on LSD. He fried his brain. He never came back to school, and the friendship disappeared. Who your child surrounds themself with is critical, whether they are in middle school, high school, or college. This is also especially true for boyfriends and girlfriends. They can have immense positive or negative influence. Get to know them. Maybe a weekend dinner invite would be in order with real conversations. One of those no texting or earphones or TV or cell phone kind of dinners.

Teach your child to absolutely help a friend if they can, but also to recognize when that friend is beyond their help and it is time to find a new friend. If that friend starts making bad decisions and can't be talked out of them, your child may have to move on. Bad decisions are ones that you would hate to have blasted on the front page of the morning newspaper. For example, you would not want to read the headline: "[Your Child's Name] caught as part of cheating ring on AP biology final...or part of drug and alcohol bust at local high school...or part of bullying squad connected to a student's suicide." These would NOT be groups of people who will help make your child better. Option-limiting influences need to be avoided. Option-enhancing influences need to be nurtured.

> **PARENT ALERT:** Are you comfortable with your child's group of friends? Is your child a positive influence on those around him/her? If you answered no to either of those questions, then you need to evaluate how you can influence your child to choose a better set of friends. How do you do that...? Help them find a new interest that captures their attention and brings a new set of friends into their world.

11. Lead and Create

Once your child has found an activity they are passionate about, go beyond just joining the group and find a way to bring leadership to that activity. Leadership could be bringing your skills to an existing organization at your school or community or could be creating something new when you find something is missing.

Let's say your child is really interested in dentistry or engineering, but there is no club on the high school campus that could help them gain information or contacts in that profession. They can create one. They can find a teacher to mentor or sponsor their group at school. I have talked to many students interested in studying medicine in college, and when I ask them whether they belong to the medical club at their school, they frequently say, "No, they don't do anything in that club." My next comment to them is, "Then fix it. If it is something you really care about, then commit and fix it." If you think there is something wrong, then there is a pretty good chance that other people are thinking the same thing. Another approach—and perhaps the ultimate form of leadership—is finding what is missing in your community and creating a solution. Does your local art museum have a teen group who works to increase teen involvement and participation in community art projects? If not, have your child approach them and suggest it.

Colleges and employers love leaders. Oftentimes in work interviews, I will ask my teen applicants to "tell me about a time you have demonstrated leadership." If your student has an interview with a highly selective college or for a scholarship or competitive summer program, this is also a question that they could get asked. Developing a leadership profile can be difficult, especially the first and second year of high school while they may still be sorting out their passions. Look for opportunities to develop that part of them, especially in areas of intense interest.

> **PARENT ALERT:** Identify a leadership opportunity with your student.

12. Make Study Skills a Habit

We have already reviewed the importance of the planner as one of the most important tools in developing study skills as habits. It can be the heart of your child effectively accomplishing the block-and-tackle (practice) part of studying. In many high schools, homework as a category of overall grade may only count for 20%, but that 20% can be the difference between a grade of a 72% (C) and a 92% (A). Your child needs to be doing all of the homework, even if they think it is boring or rote.

By the way, studying isn't just doing homework. Your student needs to create a study plan to prep for their tests as well. Your child should know exactly:

- where they are going to study (a quiet, organized area as free of noise and distractions as possible),
- when they are going to study (a two-plus hour block of time of the afternoon or evening),
- which class they are going to study first (they should attack their hardest subject first while their brain is at its most alert),
- what food and drink they will have on hand (something healthy and satiating), and
- what set of supplies they will have consistently on hand (such as pens, pencils, index cards, highlighters, computer).

Most importantly, all distractions have to be eliminated. That includes turning off the phone. What do you do when your phone buzzes? You look at it. If your child is doing the same, they are not able to focus on studying. I have had dozens of parents tell me they don't understand why Suzy is getting such bad grades because she is in her room studying for hours each night. It turns out that Suzy is actually spending most of her time playing or texting on her phone. Even if she tries to focus, the phone buzz stops all study concentration. She tries not to look but can't help herself. Even if she tries to ignore it, she is still thinking about it. After reading two whole pages, she realizes she was thinking about what's happening on her phone and doesn't remember anything she read, so she starts over. That adds up to many, many minutes being wasted. Kaput. Have your child turn off the phone when they are studying, and check that the phone is actually off. Keep checking until you are confident they can do it by themselves. A good idea would be to create a phone drawer in the kitchen where the phone stays during study time. Try it. I promise, it works.

> **PARENT ALERT:** Teach yourself and your child to TURN OFF THE PHONE when studying or doing something that requires focus.

13. Stay Fit

Your child's physical health is the foundation of their development and performance in high school. Make sure they have decent nutrition (which means eating breakfast, lunch, and dinner), stay fit by exercising or participating in sports, and, for goodness' sake, get enough sleep. Talk about the basic food groups and help them stick to it (https://www.myplate.gov/). Extreme dieting is as bad as being extremely overweight in the world of health. Moderation is an important concept in nutrition. Take time to help them know their body and what makes it strong and feel well. Also, help them be able to voice their nutritional needs. They should know your family health history, such as heart disease, diabetes, and allergies. Their best friend may be able to eat milk products and cheese like there is no tomorrow, but if your child is lactose intolerant, that may not be in their own best interests. The same goes for sugar, carbs, and gluten. They need to know their eating profile and embrace it. They are different than anyone else on the planet. They need to start recognizing how they are different and not be afraid to say, "No, I can't eat chocolate because it makes me break out and I just don't feel good after I eat it." They may be teased for it in the beginning, but everyone has something that they really shouldn't be eating.

Health issues to be aware of, including food sensitivities and family health history:

One of the biggest fears parents have about the high school experience, and rightfully so, is related to drugs and social interactions. Often, those two things go hand in hand. Keep them aware of and away from the perils of smoking, drugs, drinking, and vaping. They are everywhere. Help your child prepare and practice responses to the inevitable question: "Do you want to try this?" Their answer could be as simple as "no, because I am an athlete" or "no, because I want to go to college" or, if all else fails, "no, because I know my parents will kill me if I do." Help them find a reason and actually say it out loud. They will know someone involved with one or all of the above vices. Make sure they know why and how to resist the influence.

Be especially aware of the party situations. Make certain you know if a parent will be there AND what that parent's position is on drinking and drug use. Make sure you know exactly where they will be (the phone app "Find a Friend" can be helpful with that). You are the parent and can direct where they are allowed to go and the consequences if they don't follow your family rules. They should also know if there is a history of substance or alcohol abuse that runs in the family and should be ever more vigilant if there is. I can think of NO situation where high school drug use has ended in a positive way. Not one. Be alert and vigilant and adopt a no-tolerance policy. Look for telltale signs, like lying, needing money, depression, anxiety, and sudden shifts in grades, friends, or sleeping patterns. Get educated about all the warning signs. Contact a professional if you suspect any substance issues. The Resources section at the end of this book includes some helpful recommendations.

Mental Health

It is hard enough to be a teenager today without having to face the reality of a worldwide pandemic. Some teenagers find themselves facing very adult problems or situations without the judgement skills or experience to know what to do. Often they don't even know how to ask for help. If your child is showing signs of depression, anxiety, or has shown signs of personality changes or you are concerned that they are using illegal substances, get them help from a healthcare professional. A downward spiral can accelerate very quickly. If you see signs of unhealthy behavior such as a potential eating disorder or if your child is self-harming, get them help from a healthcare professional. Do not hesitate. Do it now.

For background information, teen suicide is higher among males than females, although females attempt suicide more than males. The CDC has documented an increase in suicide attempts due to COVID, particularly among girls. Something that has contributed to teen suicide rates in recent years has been feelings of social isolation, lack of a support network, bullying, and loss of a parent due to death or divorce. Do not think it cannot happen to your child. If the signs are there, take action. The Resource section lists several suicide hotlines that can be called. If there is an immediate threat, take them to the nearest emergency room or call 911.

> **PARENT ALERT:** Identify family and student health issues, write them down, and communicate with your child about them. Make sure THEY know why they are not going to do drugs, drink and drive, or smoke. Practice saying it out loud.

14. Show Academic Curiosity

Another way to create options is simply to develop an academic curiosity or vitality about life in general. If one is curious, one is interested and interesting. For many years, the Stanford's supplement questions section of the Common Application included questions along the line of: How have you demonstrated or proved an academic curiosity or vitality outside of school? What have you done outside of school to show a love of learning, a sustained, true, deep, genuine love of learning and knowledge? Again, we are back to the "do stuff" philosophy. Think active, not passive. What have you DEMONSTRATED... ACCOMPLISHED...WON ACCLAIM FOR? What do you do just for the sake of a love of learning?

I worked with a student who loved astronomy. There were no astronomy classes available at their high school, so they went to elite college programs at different universities each summer to learn about cosmology and the universe. They demonstrated an academic curiosity outside the classroom. I've had other students who spent their summers volunteering in a local law office or volunteering with their veterinarian. Some students have gone to night courses at the local community college to learn more about subjects like international relations. Others have spent summers in a class at their local state university learning what engineering is. The high school didn't offer a class, so they found another way to learn about something they were deeply interested in and curious about. Our youngest daughter is a writer. In her quest to find out more about the art of writing, she attended a college summer program while in high school where one of the final assignments involved sitting in an outside garden museum in front of a Rodin sculpture and writing about what it said to her. Her piece on *The Gates of Hell* was heralded by her professor and was part of the impetus for her to attend Columbia University and major in creative writing. Her first job out of college was writing for ESPN. That act of academic curiosity while in high school set her on a path for her future career.

> **PARENT ALERT:** Identify with your child at least one academic curiosity. Help them find a way to study it outside of their high school class.

15. Develop Resilience

Did you have a flawless high school experience? Make every team you tried out for? Get the lead role at every audition? Get every job you ever interviewed for? Get into every college you applied to? Avoid all drama in your home or with your friend group?

The fact that you have been through at least some of these experiences means you have brought resilience to your parenting style. Never allowing your child to be in a position to fail can mean that they will never have a bump or bruise, but how realistic is that for life? To be resilient, you have to first fall down to be able to learn about the gumption to get back up. Resilience is a characteristic that colleges prize. When life is not perfect, will this child be able to fight their way through? If your child has been in all standard track classes so that they can ace every class, what will happen when they get into college and they don't get that A? They have to learn how to work at something. If they disagree with someone, do they need "protection." As Vince Lombardi said, "It's not whether you get knocked down, it's whether you get up." We all get knocked down at some point.

If they are never stretched and only try things within their immediate grasp, you will never know—and they will never know—what they can achieve. Don't keep their ceiling too low. Let them try and show them how to get up if they fail. Adversity happens. Helping them avoid it at all costs is not the solution.

Summary

So, to create options while in high school, your student needs to:

1. Do Stuff
2. Be a Reader
3. Be Engaged
4. Study
5. Plan
6. Create Goals
7. Be Passionate
8. Find Self-Confidence
9. Utilize Resources
10. Be Surrounded by Quality People
11. Lead and Create
12. Make Study Skills a Habit
13. Stay Fit
14. Show Academic Curiosity
15. Develop Resilience

Here is something I have told students countless times over the years: In high school, most teachers and counselors and administrators really don't want to talk to your parents. When you hit 9th grade or beyond, they want to talk to YOU. Your future needs to have your voice. What do you want? What character do you represent? They want you to take responsibility for your actions and results. Parents absolutely guide and help shape and support you, but once you hit high school, you need to start developing your own direction and emphasis and be able to represent those values and communicate them to others. Do you want your parents literally coming to college with you to talk to your professors when you don't turn in work? Do you want your parent calling your professor asking for an extension on an assignment because you had a tough weekend and broke up with your girlfriend or boyfriend? Do you want your parent calling the dean of students at your college or your employer asking them to remind you daily to take your ADHD medication? Or to check your planner to make sure that you got the right assignment? How totally and completely embarrassing that would be!!!!

In high school, your child needs to start taking on the responsibilities needed for "adulting." Once they get into college or start work, you may not know if they are going to school or work every day. But your child will know, and they must accept the responsibilities that come with it. If they don't go to class, they risk failing that class and falling into academic probation or suspension, getting kicked out of school, or losing their scholarship. If they don't go to work, they will lose their job. In high school, your child needs to get in the habit of taking on those kinds of responsibilities. The choices they make will affect the options they will have at graduation.

Options Year by Year

It is stunning sometimes the misconceptions that are proliferated within high school circles and on social media about the college admission process, including the application and interview. The kids for the most part don't know what the directors of admissions are looking for and get some very upside-down views of what is important. They follow each other around in a downward spiral of misinformation that is sometimes almost comical. Make sure you know what is important and can explain to them why it is important.

The next four sections focus on how to create options in each specific high school grade level and are presented as if YOU, the parent, are talking directly to your high school student.

CHAPTER 3

FRESHMAN YEAR

Get Great Grades (G3)

Your grade history starts the first day of your freshman year of high school. In fact, some students can use high school–level class grades from middle school as part of their high school transcript in certain states. For example, some states allow you to take an algebra 1 class from 8th grade as high school algebra 1 class credit. It could count as part of your high school GPA. Freshman year can be tough academically as there will potentially be many more classes and teachers than you had in middle school. The level of difficulty will be greater. You are expected to perform with a higher level of rigor than before. Plan on studying two to three hours per night, meaning:

- doing homework,
- reading assigned books with annotation/underlining/ highlighting,
- reviewing or rewriting your notes,
- studying and memorizing items studied that day in class,

- studying material that you will be tested on later,
- looking at what is due that week, reviewing your schedule, and determining when you will work on assignments and study for tests, and
- keeping your backpack organized.

College Research

If you think you are college bound, identify three colleges that you would like to visit. A good starting point would be colleges that are nearby or in-state. Before visiting, review what would be required on that school's application in terms of GPA and SAT/ACT scores. Remember, your high school GPA calculation starts your freshman year. If you need a 3.0 GPA to get into your in-state college, that means a B average. A 3.5 GPA is half As in core classes and half Bs unweighted. A weighted GPA is one where a student gets additional GPA points for difficult classes (honors, IB, AP, dual enrollment). An unweighted GPA tops out at 4.0, where an A equals 4.0, B equals 3.0, C equals 2.0, etc.

Also, know how your colleges view a D or F in a class. Many colleges will say that a D or F does not represent mastery of the topic and they will not acknowledge completion of the class. Ds are usually considered passing by the high school, and you will get high school credit for high school graduation...but a college may not view it as mastery of the topic and may not give you credit for that class. I usually HIGHLY RECOMMEND that a student retake any class where they receive a D or F, both for increased comprehension of the topic and for your GPA and options after high school. Also, difficulty in a class increases each year. If you get a D or F in an algebra 1 class, your chances of doing well in algebra 2 are greatly diminished. Don't accept something that could be setting you up for future failure. Many high schools will let you retake a couple of semesters' worth of classes online or during the summer. Do NOT make it a habit though. Recovery or remediation of classes does have limits… and could mean you going to school year-round. It could mean saying goodbye to other options for your summer breaks. It can work as an emergency plan you occasionally fall back on but not something to fall back on all the time.

Three colleges I will visit this year:

1.

2.

3.

Take a full tour of the campus, whether that is virtually or in person. Start a college notebook and write down your impressions of each university. What did you like? What didn't you like? Think about things like size of the school, weather, and closeness to home. Some students like the idea of being close to home. Many students feel like they are ready to leave the nest and want to move away. That feeling may develop and change over the next four years.

We need to have a serious conversation about finances and how that will impact your decisions about college. Will you need merit or financial need scholarships in order to attend? Is there a certain amount of money that has been, can, or will be set aside for college attendance? How much are we willing to take on in terms of college debt to attend? How much money are you willing to put aside? These are realistic, MATURE conversations that need to happen. Some students with limited family financial resources will plan on going to a community college for a year or two and then transfer to an in-state school. This option could save the financially strapped family tens of thousands of dollars. In this scenario, many students save money on room and board by living at home as well as paying up to one-tenth the tuition.

Most in-state schools have a strong transfer program for credits earned at community and state college. If you want to research this option, you should also look into what classes are transferrable. Community colleges often have a smaller environment than large public college campuses. Some high schools offer dual enrollment classes while you are in high school, meaning you get high school credit AND community college or college credit at the same time. There is usually an additional fee for these classes and sometimes some basic tests for placement, but you get both (dual) high school and college credit. At least some out-of-state or private schools accept community college credits. Even if they do not, the directors of admissions will take into account that you enrolled in classes beyond a standard track high school class. With these schools, you may not get college credit, but you do get the recognition for the rigor of those classes, which will be factored into their admissions decision. Usually, AP and IB classes are thought to be even more rigorous than community college classes.

During your freshman year, do some projections of what you might be taking for your four years in high school, semester by semester. You may find that you will have to be taking classes in the summer to fulfill all the classes your dream school requires. It's best to know that early than to make an unexpected discovery in your junior year.

If you are not sure if you are going to be college bound, discuss post-graduation options with your parents and research what would be required for each of those options.

> **PARENT ALERT:** Have the what-are-your-plans-after-high-school conversation with your child. Discuss college vs. no college vs. community college vs. trade school. If your child is college bound, visit three schools, discuss financial options, and reinforce the importance of getting great grades starting their freshman year. If they are not college bound, explore other options and what would be required.

Know the Rules and Consequences

Make certain you know the rules and consequences of actions while in high school. Each school has different policies, and you need to know what the rules AND consequences are for your school. Ignorance of the rules is no excuse. Some important questions to consider include:

- What are the consequences of cheating, and what does your school consider to be cheating?

- What are the penalties for vaping, smoking, and alcohol or drug use?
- What is considered bullying and sexual harassment, how should they be reported, and what are the penalties?
- What is considered a dress code violation?
- What are the penalties for theft allegations, destruction of school property, and fighting?
- How many days can be missed each quarter/semester before you are expelled? (Hint: it may be fewer than you think.)
- How is extensive tardiness viewed and what are the consequences?
- What is the difference between detention, in-school suspension, out-of-school suspension, and expulsion? How does each show up on your school record?

	SCHOOL CONSEQUENCES	PARENT CONSEQUENCES
Cheating		
Alcohol Use		
Drug Use		
Vaping/Smoking		
Bullying		

Sexual Harassment		
Fighting		
Destroying School Property		
Theft		
Dress Code Violations		
Excessive Absence		
Excessive Tardiness		

Students at a private Catholic school were suspended for posting pictures on Facebook of a group of students drinking beer at an after-school, off-campus party. Why would they be suspended when that happened outside of school? Well, they were wearing school uniforms in the picture and were thus viewed as being representatives of the school while they were engaged in illegal activity. Those suspensions became part of their permanent record.

Rules can change, so it is a good thing to review each year. Parents also need to know and understand these rules. Take the time to read them together. The decisions that you make in these areas can be option creating or option killing.

In terms of absences, tardies, and missing school for doctor's appointments, make sure you and your parents know how to comply with these reporting requirements. Mistakes in these areas can affect your school record. Look up the procedures and the following contact information for your school so that when situations come up, you are ready. Program these numbers and email addresses into your phones.

	SCHOOL CONTACT INFORMATION
School front desk	
School counselor	
School nurse	
Reporting an absence	

If your school has an app that allows you to check grades, make sure you and your parents have downloaded it and make sure you have access to transcript information. Sometimes mistakes creep onto transcripts with incorrect grades or mandatory high school testing reporting, and it is best to catch them right away. It happened with two of our daughters, and thankfully we caught them quickly. Otherwise, those mistakes could have caused significant problems down the line when it is too late to fix.

> **PARENT ALERT:** Know how to report an absence, tardiness, or a need to miss part of the school day for a doctor or dental appointment. Do not forget to comply with these reporting requirements. Program the school numbers into your phone so you have the information handy and so you don't accidentally ignore any calls from the school.

Do Stuff

Explore your interests. If you don't know what your interests really are, then this is the PERFECT time to try new things: a new sport, the debate team, theatre, a musical instrument, the robotics team, a school club, writing, taking a coding class. Just put yourself out there and try something new. If you are not sure about what you are interested in, try going to a museum and seeing if there is something there that catches your interest. Or explore different books at the library or online that may be of interest. Or try out for a sport. If you have found your passion in life, then start to become really proficient at it. Go deep. That may mean coaching it, composing it, creating within it, or volunteering to help others with it. Doing stuff will help you decide what you are interested in and may help you define a path for leadership in that area later.

One of the items definitely included in that "Do Stuff" category is READ.

> **PARENT ALERT:** Discuss the "do stuff" options with your child and facilitate attendance and participation in their chosen interests.

Take the PSAT

If your high school offers the PSAT during your freshman year, take it. There is a lot to gain and little to lose. The math sections will be slightly easier than your junior year PSAT, but it gives you a sense of what the SAT experience will be like. It allows you to see how your brain holds up for a two-hour, 45-minute testing period. It lets you see what the expectations are of the SAT, which is looking at your critical thinking skills. Get a baseline and see how you compare to other freshmen. This gives you more information on your general preparedness. If your reading scores are below the 75th percentile range, you may want to consider bolstering your reading comprehension skills now. It is the hardest section of a standardized test to turn around in a short period of time. Understanding nuance takes work. Knowing the difference between "an answer" and "the best answer" takes time. Your math core knowledge will grow with time, but unless you are reading on a regular basis, reading skills will not experience this same natural growth.

Start a Resume

Resumes are a summary of all of your experiences and achievements. This is a living document, meaning that it needs to be updated often, at least every semester. You should be adding to your list of activities and accomplishments regularly, especially if you are living the "DO STUFF" mantra. An academic resume is slightly different from a work resume. In a work resume, you are highlighting the skills that you feel will be of interest to a future employer. With an academic resume, you are highlighting the items that would be of most interest to a college director of admissions or director of scholarship fund. Again, the strongest indication of academic success in college is academic success in rigorous classes while in high school.

Academic Achievements

Not all of these will be relevant to your freshman year, but over time, you will want to highlight your overall GPA (weighted and unweighted), SAT or ACT scores (whichever is strongest), PSAT scores (if you reach a level of excellence on this test that puts you in the National Merit Commended or higher level), list of AP or IB classes and AP test scores (if scores are 4 or 5 for AP), capstone classes, any extensive research project that you may have done with a brief description, and class rank or percentage (if your school calculates it). You want to let the director of admissions know that you are capable of handling the academic environment at their college. They do not want to admit you and have you fail, be put on academic probation, or drop out. They want a strong, robust community of bright, curious students.

Leadership

As a freshman, you may not have a lot to add to this section, but you need to know that it is an important element of increasing your college options. As you continue through your high school journey, you need to look for opportunities or create opportunities in areas of interest where you can demonstrate leadership. These might include running for a position on your school's student council or a school club that interests you. Other examples at school could be through your high school newspaper, yearbook, music, theater, or sports. You can also look for leadership skill development programs within your community as well: YMCA/YWCA, Boys and Girls Club, Rotary Clubs, Junior Achievement, civic programs through the mayor's office, police or fire departments, hospitals, senior centers, art museums, science centers, and places of worship. Think about being consistent with your leadership development pursuits and your future major. In the resume, you want to provide a brief description of your leadership position responsibilities including money raised, number of people helped or managed, number of hours of participation, and years of participation. These should be listed in the order of importance to you, not necessarily chronological order. Lead with your strongest leadership participation.

Honors and Awards

These are the areas where you have demonstrated excellence. Heads up: if you have Ivy League colleges on your list, you will be competing against students who have international and national awards for excellence. This section could include international, national, state, city, county, or school awards. Boy or Girl Scouts should list the highest award received. This section can include awards from academic competitions, National Merit or Commended status, and rankings for theater, vocal, band, or sports. Again, these should be in order of importance to you.

For creative students reading this section, I know that it is hard to put yourself out there with your work. For many, creating art is like exposing a piece of their soul, and nobody wants to have it criticized or risk being rejected. Take a look at Scholastic's Art and Writing Awards program (www.artandwriting.org). There are many different categories and award levels. I had the opportunity to work with one of the national award winners in poetry who ended up attending Brown University. And I have worked with several Gold and Silver Key winners who have also gone to Ivy League schools like Columbia University. This is a well-regarded, respected program with lots of opportunities for varying levels of recognition. So, for my artistic readers…try it.

Community Service

In this section, you want to provide a brief description of your community service activities, including the hours of participation per year. It should also include the amount of money raised and the approximate number of people aided. Initially, you may try several different community service programs until you find one that "speaks" to you and your values. Once you have made that discovery, think about focusing your energies to help develop that organization. In the big picture of community service, 25 hours in one area is better than 5 hours of participation in five different organizations. It shows commitment and depth. There is also a national award for community service through the President's Volunteer Service Award program (www. presidentialserviceawards.gov). Many newspapers list community service organizations that are looking for help, and faith-based organizations often have programs with which you can get involved.

Athletics

This section includes both school and non-school athletics. If you play a sport, indicate whether it is at the club, varsity, or junior varsity level and the number of years and position played. Generally, high school resumes only include accomplishments achieved while in high school (not middle school), but if you have played a sport for 12 years, you want to include those years and get recognition for your level of depth and involvement with the sport. If your team has won any awards, put those in the "Honors and Awards" section. If you have made a national or state team in your sport or have made "cuts" of a specific level, that could also be included in the award section. I have worked with students who have been to Olympic Trials and the Olympics while they are still in high school. In fact, one young lady represented Canada and actually won several medals at the Olympics.

Don't forget to include non-school sports, like martial arts, archery, skiing, scuba diving, sailing, crew, figure skating, gymnastics. I worked with one young lady who had an unusual list of island locations she had visited. When I asked her why she had been to those places, she just said she was on vacation there with her parents. When her mother came to pick her up, I chatted with her about their vacation plans for the next summer and she said their family was going to Belize. It turns out the daughter I had just been working with was a Master PADI-certified diver. She did wreck diving, night diving, rescue diving, and cave diving, and, on top of that, she trained diving trainers how to train diving. When I asked the student why she hadn't thought to include that on her resume, she just said that it didn't fit into any of the categories and she didn't think that being a master diver would be interesting to colleges. On the contrary, it spoke volumes of her personality, depth, and spirit and gave even more credibility as to why she wanted to be a marine biologist.

Performing Arts

This would be for serious involvement with multiple years of performance history. It includes drama, musical theater, instruments, voice, vocal training, dance training, comedy, impromptu, slam poetry, speech, debate, or any performance craft. If you are involved in theater art, include shows you have performed in, year, and parts played or role on the set. If you are working with civic or community theater groups, this would also be the place to list it. I worked with one young lady who was part of an Equity mentorship program that would allow her to get her Equity card (membership to a national theater group) before she went off to school in New York. If you have gone through specific training, list it here: special summer camps, X years of classical or operatic training with Master Baritone X, composing training, multiple instruments played, international singing trips, etc. If you are a musician working on a particularly difficult piece, list it. If you have a favorite genre of music or composer, list them. This piece of information can give a person a better sense of your personality. As an example, if you tell someone that your favorite composer is Tchaikovsky, then the reader might think big personality…canons, fire, red flares, big music. That is very different than someone who prefers the intricate, densely noted music from Mozart. If you just casually play a musical instrument or sing in a class, you may want to list it in the "Special Interests" section of your resume.

Clubs

This section can act as a punctuation point for your interests. Be careful about "serial" clubbing. These are students who belong to 15 different clubs but do not take on any leadership roles. Initially, you may need to join several clubs to find out what you are really interested in, but once you have discovered what makes your heart fly, focus your time and energy on that specific interest. National Honor Society (NHS) is a nationally recognized club that demonstrates academic prowess and usually has a community service requirement as well. For students interested in elite, highly selective colleges, NHS membership may not be a differentiating asset as most students applying to these high-end schools will be members, but you should still consider becoming a member to punctuate the value you place on academic excellence.

Work Experience

This section is especially important if you are telling a college that you are interested in majoring in business. Having worked with many students who are interested in entrepreneurship, I have been amazed at some of the businesses that they have started while still in high school, including dog walkers, cat sitters, babysitters, and tutors. I worked with a student who would go to elderly people's homes to help set up computer systems and programs and a student who painted portraits of family pets or a family home from a photograph. Another student I worked with created designs for T-shirts, and by the time he graduated, his business included hundreds of orders, including international orders. A couple of young men had websites where they sold new tennis shoes. A brother-sister team started a nonprofit organization that brought money and school supplies to a small rural village in India; there was a woman in the village they had spent multiple summers with who was revered as a healing saint. The young lady's college admission essay was stunning.

Other things that could be included in work experiences would be internships (paid or unpaid) and "shadowing" experiences. A shadowing experience is where a student spends a day, week, or longer watching what a professional does in an area that they think they might be interested in pursuing in college. Often you will see shadowing experiences in healthcare with professionals such as doctors, dentists, veterinarians, and physical therapists. In the nursing profession, I have worked with several students who actually earned their certified nursing assistant certification while in high school. Some interesting programs exist that extensively train students to work with hospice organizations and teen suicide help lines, and being a lifeguard often involves a decent amount of training. I have worked with some students who went on mission trips to foreign countries with doctors who were vaccinating parts of the village populations that they visited. For example, one young lady went on a mission trip with her Catholic high school to an orphanage and wrote an insightful college admission essay on learning what true selflessness means. She told the story how she brought a care package of supplies for a young orphan, who insisted on sharing with the other children in the orphanage; he only took the bare minimum that he needed of toothpaste, soap, and sweets and insisted that his friends should share in his "bounty." She described how she brought that spirit back to her high school and wove it into her life going forward. She ended up accepting an offer from Texas Christian University.

Special Interests

Finally, your resume should have a section on special interests. This is by no means a throwaway section. Rather, it is your opportunity to give some insight into your personality. Are you a sudoku master or juggler? Do you enjoy cooking or baking, and do you have a signature dish? Have you had unusual travel experiences, and do you speak any additional languages? Are you certified in first aid or CPR? Do you collect anything? This section helps give your resume dimension and spice. Think of it as an opportunity to make yourself even more memorable to the person reading your resume.

For a sample resume, check out the Sophomore section. Keep in mind that, as a freshman, you may not have a lot of "meat on the bones" with your initial resume. That's okay; it is still never too early to start. And don't underestimate who you are or what you can do while you are in high school.

PARENT ALERT: Create a joint exercise with your child to put their initial resume on paper and use it as a tool for freshman year goal setting. Together, outline the actual resume at the beginning of freshman year, then have them create a "goal version." In other words, what do they want to add or accomplish by the end of the year in each category? Then, have them pin the goal resume in a place where both of you can see it every day. It may be a bit overwhelming at first, but it's exhilarating when you go back to it at the end of the year and realize how much they have accomplished. This exercise becomes an incredible opportunity to talk and listen to your child and discover their true interests.

FRESHMAN BEGINNING-YEAR RESUME

Academic:
Leadership:
Honors and Awards:
Community Service:

Athletic:
Performing Arts:
Clubs:
Work Experience:
Special Interests:

FRESHMAN YEAR-END RESUME GOALS

Academic Goals:
Leadership Goals:
Honors and Awards Goals:

Community Service Goals:
Athletic Goals:
Performing Arts Goals:
Club Goals:
Work Experience Goals:
Special Interest Goals

Create a High School "Bucket List"

Most bucket lists deal with things that you want to do before you die…but let's keep that more manageable and make it the things that you want to do before you graduate from high school. Focus on 12 things, or 3 things each year of high school. You can think of several different categories to keep the lists in, such as:

Places I want to go:

Things I want to hear:

Things I want to see:

Foods I want to eat:

Books I want to read:

Things I want to do:

Things I want to learn:

Sports or physical activities I want to try:

The thing I want to learn more about:

Put pictures of the things on that list around your room so you can see them every day. For some of these, you may have to find a way to make money to achieve them. If you get an allowance, maybe save some of it for your bucket list. Maybe do some additional chores around the neighborhood for money. You may be able to get a part-time job as well if you can handle having one and still perform well in your academics. Or maybe you can make something to sell. Talk with your parents and share your list. They may be able to help you with some of the items.

> **PARENT ALERT:** Put your "coach" hat on and encourage your student to do the bucket list exercise. Help them sort through and prioritize ideas. Make sure each chosen item is affordable, practical, and achievable.

Do Something Amazing with Your Summer

Summer is a time to continue accomplishment...not to stop learning or growing. Some summer activities may only be a week or two at a time, like classes or workshops, so you can often string many things together. Yes, you can continue to read during the summer even when the reading is not assigned from school. Some honors classes may have required reading during the summer anyway. If you did not do well in classes (meaning you earned a D or F, or maybe even a C, depending on your college goals), then summer is the time to retake those classes.

Summer may also be a great time to identify something you want to get "better" at. Of course, you will need to define better...

faster, stronger, improved efficiency…whatever better means to you. You need to define it so that you know when you have accomplished your goal. One of my daughters returned from a creative writing summer camp having a portfolio of work. The next summer, she went to a summer camp where she became a published author in a summer literary journal from that college. Both summer experiences sparked an interest that has stayed with her until this day.

Conclusion

If you can do these things your freshman year, you will start developing choices and options for yourself.

> **PARENT ALERT:** Remember, you are not your child's friend. They may want summer to be just a time for rest and play—don't let that happen! It's okay to be the bad guy here. Encourage the ideas above and ensure the close of their freshman year includes an amazing summer.

CHAPTER 4

SOPHOMORE YEAR

PARENT ALERT: Sophomore year tends to be a bit easier after the trials of freshman year. Your child may have a bit more time to get involved in outside activities. However, it is *very* important they never take their eye off the academic ball. Sophomore year is also a critical social year. Pay attention to who they are spending time with. Listen. Trust but verify. Encourage the joint exercise of reviewing freshman year accomplishments and updating the resume and sophomore goals.

Continue to Get Great Grades (and Stretch Yourself)

If you aren't already in advanced or honors classes, you need to start thinking about how you could further invest yourself in more rigorous classes that you are interested in. Some sophomore students may be in pre-IB curriculum from their freshman year, some may already be in an honors track of classes, and even some may be in AP classes. Think about what classes you may want to start to demonstrate a passion in. Not all students can handle a full honors schedule, so think about focusing on the classes that are most interesting to you or where you usually do well. Teachers may also be able to steer you in the right direction and help you identify classes where you will be able to advance. Yes, you may have to work harder in these classes, but you need to think about stretching yourself.

Continue to Attack Your Bucket & Do Stuff Lists

The three things from my DO STUFF list that I will accomplish this year are:

Fall Semester:

1.

2.

3.

Spring Semester:

1.

2.

3.

Places I want to go:
Things I want to hear:
Things I want to see:
Foods I want to eat:
Books I want to read:
Things I want to do:
Things I want to learn:
Sports or physical activities I want to try:
The thing I want to learn more about:

Take the PSAT/PLAN (again)

Many high schools offer sophomore students the option to take the PSAT 9/10 and/or PLAN (pre-ACT) during their sophomore year. If you took one of these tests your freshman year, take it again and give it your best; when you compare it to your baselines scores, you will be able to see if you improved in any areas. If you didn't have an opportunity to get that baseline score during your freshman year, now is the time. Look for areas where you are performing lower than the 75th percentile mark compared to your peers on a national level. Those are areas where you need to get help to increase your options after graduation. If you are scoring lower on reading compared to your peers, it will affect not only your test scores but also your ability to do well in school. If you are not proficient at reading, it will impact your ability to get good grades while in high school, perform on tests to get into the military, attend certain colleges, and get a job. These tests help identify strengths and weaknesses. It then becomes your responsibility to seek out help in areas where you need extra support.

The PSAT is not a college admissions test, but it does give you a heads-up in areas to start to prepare for. If your PSAT score from your sophomore year is over 1250, you may be in a position to consider preparing for the possibility of competing for the National Merit Scholarship Program when you take the test your junior year. Whether you qualify as a National Merit Scholar is dependent on your index score from your PSAT, which is a specific way of converting your score by moving section scores one decimal place, doubling the reading/writing score, and adding it to the math score; essentially, the reading scores count twice as much as the math score. Because of the way the index score is calculated, it is possible to have two students have the same overall PSAT tests scores and to have one qualify for the National Merit Program and the other one not to qualify for the program, depending on their reading/writing scores. National Merit qualifying scores are different every year and also vary by state, and there are separate scores for international participants. The qualifying score for the National Merit Scholarship only counts your junior year, not your freshman or sophomore years. But you do want to know how you are doing compared to your peers, and if you are approaching a National Merit–level score your sophomore year, you want to consider beginning your preparation for that process.

Continue to Visit Colleges

If you can't visit the colleges due to financial or other constraints, then research them online. Most students get a richer picture of a campus when it is unfiltered, but if you can't physically visit, then go to the website and understand what kinds of programs they have that you might be interested in: research opportunities, foreign campuses, internship opportunities, majors, professors, classes, etc. Take notes. Know what is important in their admissions process. Most colleges will tell you. Don't be surprised if GPA in rigorous classes is high on the list. Some schools will put more emphasis on letters of recommendation than others. Many will look to test scores; however, there are hundreds of colleges that belong to the FairTest list, meaning they don't look at test scores. Some schools take a much more holistic look, and applicants get high points for leadership, excellence awards, and the ability to communicate who they are through their essay. Some colleges have special buckets for underrepresented minorities, special financial situations, and legacy families. See if you can find alumnae from the schools you are most interested in through family, friends, siblings of friends, teachers, extended family, graduates from your high school, and counselors. Reach out to those individuals and ask them about their experiences. Most importantly, start your research now!

> *Three colleges I will visit this year:*
>
> 1.
>
> 2.
>
> 3.

Update Your Resume

Remember, your resume is a living, breathing document and it should change and grow every year...because every year you are going to be doing things to grow. Compare this version with your freshman version and your end-of-freshman-year-goal version. How did you do? Now, update your end-of-year sophomore version and make sure your goals are obtainable and that you are stretching yourself!!!! Use the sample format provided:

Resume Sample Format

This is a sample format of a resume style recommended for students to be considered for scholarships, letters of recommendation, and college applications. Your academic resume can exceed one page to adequately communicate the depth and breadth of your involvement. Make sure to include duties, responsibilities, and/ or project involvement where applicable.

Name
Address
Email
Cell Phone

ACADEMICS:
Overall GPA: (Show both weighted and unweighted)
Class Rank:
IB or AP student and classes (if applicable):
SAT or ACT Score:

HONORS & AWARDS:
Name of Award   Year Received:
Indicate top awards, honors, and scholarships at the national, state, city, county, or school level. Include involvement in Boy Scouts and Girl Scouts at the highest level achieved. Include National Merit or Commended distinction, academic competitions, and superior rankings for theater, vocal, band, etc. Do not include "Who's Who" type of awards received in the mail.

LEADERSHIP:
Name of Organization, Title   Years/Hours:
Provide a brief description of leadership role. Include leadership roles in such activities as student council, national honor society, high school newspaper, yearbook, music/vocal, sports, clubs, etc. Include leadership roles in a volunteer activity such as "lead instructor" in your faith-based community.

COMMUNITY SERVICE:
Name of Organization: Years/Hours:
Provide a brief description of community service activities. List only those activities where you contributed over 25 hours with one organization.

ATHLETICS:
Type of Sport (Indicate Varsity or JV):   Year:
*If Captain/Co-Captain, indicate under **Leadership** as well.*

PERFORMING ARTS:
Type: Year:
*If you held a leadership role such as Section Leader, Captain, Drum Major – indicate under **Leadership** as well. Include names of productions if applicable and your role.*

CLUBS:
Type: Year:
*Describe club activities: indicate whether you held a leadership role. If so, make sure that leadership role is indicated under **Leadership** as well.*

WORK EXPERIENCE:
Position, Employer, Hours Per Week: Year:
Brief description of your responsibilities.

SPECIAL INTERESTS:
Do you play an instrument or have a hobby? Include it here. Also, include anything special or unique about you personally.

Do Something Doubly Amazing

In the summer between your sophomore and junior years, do something that is amazing and consistent with your interests. Many elite summer programs are competitive and may have deadline dates for applications that are in December or January of your sophomore year. Take the action needed to complete the application. Get ahead of those dates. At the beginning of your sophomore year, do some planning on what you would like to be doing next summer and share them with your support network (parents, counselors, extended family, friends, siblings). I know some students who have spent a summer on a research ship at sea and others who have spent time volunteering to help in local or national parks. Get out of your comfort zone or dive more deeply into your passion.

Know How You Are "Weird"

"Don't waste any time trying to be like anybody but yourself, because the things that make you strange are the things that make you powerful." – Ben Platt, Tony Award Acceptance Speech, 2017, Best Actor in a Musical, for *Dear Evan Hansen* on Broadway.

Write down what is "weird" about you...and do something about it. Make sure you are doing things that demonstrate your unique interest. Look for and seek out leadership opportunities in those areas of interest. Don't be afraid to create something new. DON'T BE AFRAID TO DIFFERENTIATE YOURSELF. In middle school, most students strive to be the same as everyone else. They don't want to stand out and be different. They believe if they are "like" everyone else they will be "liked" more and will fit in. What you should know by now is that your differences are your strengths. Your power is in your "difference," not in your "sameness." One of the questions frequently asked in the college admissions supplemental sections is: "What special skill or talent or perspective will you be bringing to our college campus/community?" Being different has value. Start to be able to articulate, embrace, and develop your special differences. Embrace your weirdness.

My weirdness is:

My parents think my weirdness is:

PARENT ALERT: It is very important to encourage this conversation about your child's uniqueness. Help your student truly see and value their individual strengths. This is a critical step to them embracing their superpower.

Get Certified

If you are interested in medicine, get CPR and first aid and defibrillator certified or certified as a lifeguard or as a babysitter. If you are interested in marine biology, get scuba certified. If you are interested in computer programming, get certified in an aspect of programing. If you are interested in business, get Excel certified. Take classes outside of school that demonstrate an interest and level of proficiency in that area. I worked with one young lady who actually got EMT certified while in high school. She did late-night ride-alongs with EMT professionals and took the test, all during the COVID pandemic. She told stories of being attacked by emergency patients whom she was trying to help and using her high school knowledge of Spanish to help non-English–speaking patients. She is one of the very remarkable young people I had the honor of working with over the years.

And, although it isn't exactly a certification, one of the very biggest happenings during a student's sophomore or junior year is the ability to get a driver's license. It is important to understand that driving a car is a privilege, not a rite of passage. Be prepared to demonstrate to your parents that you are capable of handling that responsibility and balancing it with the other responsibilities you have.

Create a Driving Contract

PARENT ALERT: Your child needs to earn the right to learn how to drive and you need to hold them responsible. Be very clear about what the student has to have demonstrated to earn the right to drive. It is not a rite of passage. It is something they need to earn the right to do, similar to having to earn the right to have a cell phone in middle school. There are many responsibilities that you have as a parent in terms of a driving contract. The American Academy of Pediatrics (https://www.healthychildren. org/English/ages-stages/teen/safety/Pages/Teen-Driving-Agreement.aspx) has a parent-teen driving contract that is worth considering.

Parent-Teen Driving Agreement

I, _____, will drive carefully and cautiously and will be courteous to other drivers, bicyclists, and pedestrians at all times.

I promise that I will obey all the rules of the road.

- Always wear a seat belt and make all my passengers buckle up
- Obey all traffic lights, stop signs, other street signs, and road markings
- Stay within the speed limit and drive safely
- Never use the car to race or to try to impress others
- Never give rides to hitchhikers

I promise that I will make sure I can stay focused on driving.

- Drive with both hands on the wheel
- Never eat, drink, or use a cell phone to talk or text while I drive
- Drive only when I am alert and in emotional control
- Call my parents for a ride home if I am impaired in any way that
- interferes with my ability to drive safely
- Never use earphones to listen to electronic devices while I drive

I promise that I will respect laws about drugs and alcohol.

- Drive only when I am alcohol and drug free
- Never allow any alcohol or illegal drugs in the car
- Be a passenger only with drivers who are alcohol and drug free

I promise that I will be a responsible driver.

- Drive only when I have permission to use the car and I will not let anyone else drive the car unless I have permission
- Drive someone else's car only if I have parental permission
- Pay for all traffic citations or parking tickets
- Complete my family responsibilities and maintain good grades at school as listed here:_____

  _____

- Contribute to the costs of gasoline, maintenance, and insurance as listed here: _____

  _____

_____

_____
_____

Adapted from the American Academy of Pediatrics "Parent-Teen Driving Agreement"

Additional Promises:

I agree to the following restrictions, but understand that these restrictions will be modified by my parents as I get more driving experience and demonstrate that I am a responsible driver.

- For the next _____ months, I will not drive after _____ p.m.
- For the next _____ months, I will not transport more than _____ teen passengers (unless I am supervised by a responsible adult).
- For the next _____ months, I won't adjust the stereo, electronic devices, or air conditioning/heater while the car is moving.
- For the next _____ months, I will not drive in bad weather.
- I understand that I am not permitted to drive to off-limit locations or on roads and highways as listed here:
- Additional restrictions:

I agree to follow all the rules and restrictions in this contract. I understand that my parents will impose penalties (see below), including removal of my driving privileges, if I violate the contract.

I also understand that my parents will allow me greater driving privileges as I become more experienced and as I demonstrate that I am always a safe and responsible driver.

Penalties for contract violations

- Drove after drinking alcohol or using drugs No driving for _____ months
- Got ticket for speeding or moving violation No driving for _____ months
- Drove after night driving curfew No driving for _____ weeks/months
- Drove too many passengers No driving for _____ weeks/months
- Broke promise about seat belts (self and others) No driving for _____ weeks/months
- Drove on a road or to an area that is off-limits No driving for _____ weeks/months

Signatures

Driver: _____ Date: _____
Parent promise: I also agree to drive safely and to be an excellent role model.
Parent (or guardian): _____ Date: _____
Parent (or guardian): _____ Date: _____

From: HealthyChildren.org, "Parent-Teen Driving Agreement," American Academy of Pediatrics, https://www.healthychildren.org/English/ages-stages/teen/ safety/Pages/Teen-Driving-Agreement.aspx.

Once they get their driver's license, a lot changes. You may have even less time with them than you did before. They are truly learning how to fly. Make sure your child is ready for the responsibility based on their maturity, not just their age. The contract above helps start the discussion about your expectations and family requirements. The biggest part of the requirement on your part is certainly to always know the who, what, when, where, and why when they are not with you and "trust but verify" as appropriate. It is your responsibility as a parent to ask. Verify every once in a while until you are comfortable that they are consistently where they tell you they are, what they are doing, who they are with, and when they will be home. Hopefully, they will get to the point that they offer the information before even leaving. The cell phone app Find My Friend can also be helpful in verifying that what they are telling you and what they are actually doing is consistent.

Job?

Should my child get a job in high school? That all depends on the child, the family, and the story your child is building. Some families need their child to work. Some will make them pay their own cell phone bills or car insurance or even contribute to car payments. That is obviously a family decision. Jobs may not be a requirement for getting into college, but it depends on what direction they are going in. Some students just don't have time because of pursuits of other passions. Don't take a passion away from them just so they can check the "I had a job" box. On the other hand, there are lots of responsibilities and character that can be achieved by having a job. Some will have a job in the summer or part of the weekend.

Is there something else that they could be doing that would be a better learning experience for them? It's not just about academic learning; it's also a little of life learning as well. I know several students who, with the wonder of the internet, have started their own business as early as their sophomore year. Help them do it right, though: taxes, budgets, marketing plan, legal company entity, competitive review, etc. If that is what they want to do, have them give you a *Shark Tank*–like sales pitch. If they can't convince you, who can they convince? If they are successful in getting a job, just make sure you know what they are doing with the money. Even if they don't have a job but are receiving some type of allowance, make sure you know where that money goes too.

At the end of sophomore year, get an unofficial copy of their transcript, which you can normally get from their counselor or registrar or online. Check to make sure that everything on that record is correct. Make sure any classes that they may have taken or retaken are on the transcript and properly reflected. Mistakes happen, so get them fixed NOW. I also recommend that you do this in their junior year. For some, this year or next may also be a time for getting their driver's license and a job. Hopefully, they can maintain that stellar GPA and these other new additions to their lives.

CHAPTER 5

JUNIOR YEAR

Yikes! Junior year is by far the hardest year of high school. To begin, your classes become more rigorous, and some of you may even be taking college-level classes (dual enrollment, AP, IB, capstone). It is also the last set of grades that many colleges will see before making an admissions decision, as many of you will be applying to college or other programs before you have any of your senior year semester or quarter grades. For this reason, many colleges will look particularly closely at your grades from your junior year to truly have an idea of how you will perform in rigorous classes.

Get Great(er) Grades

Push yourself academically this year to get to your best possible overall cumulative GPA. You should have college options if your cumulative academic unweighted GPA is 3.0 in your academic classes and you have no deficiencies (Ds or Fs) in core academic classes. Of course, you will have more options with a 3.2 and even more with a 3.5 or 3.75 or above. You will want and need that level of competency as base knowledge for your college-level classes.

Academic Expectations

If you are college bound, the bare minimum GPA should be 3.0 unweighted, not including PE. The unweighted 3.0 should be reflective of core academic classes. Generally, GPAs are calculated out to two decimal points (e.g., 3.75).

Honors, AP, IB, and Dual Enrollment Classes

To be competitive for highly selective colleges, you need to be taking the hardest academic schedule available at your high school. Ivy League schools will have applicants with 10-plus AP (Advanced Placement) level classes completed upon graduation. If your high school does not offer AP classes, it will not be held against you in the application process. Acing college admissions tests would be another way of demonstrating the veracity of your academic preparation when advanced classes are not available.

Dual enrollment courses can also sometimes be an option. To be able to offer a dual enrollment class, the teacher must be certified to teach the class at a community college and high school level. Students will often have to take a test to "place" into the class. Some colleges will also give college credit for some AP classes if the student takes the AP test for the class in May and scores at a certain level. Tests are scored 1-5 with a score of 3 considered passing. Some highly selective colleges will require a 5 in order to give credit. You have to check on a class-by-class basis on the college's website, though, because some colleges will only offer credit for certain AP classes and others will require one score for credit for one class and require a higher score for credit for another class. Even if the college does not give credit for AP classes, it does demonstrate that, in high school, the student took a rigorous college-level class and hopefully did well with it. It shows an interest or curiosity or vitality in the topic beyond an average requirement. It will also help with building critical thinking or analytic skills that will help with college admissions tests.

The same can be said for International Baccalaureate (IB) classes. Not all high schools are IB program certified, however. Generally, IB classes are taken as a series of integrated classes with their own set of objectives and testing requirements, usually beginning with two years of pre-IB classes completed during your freshman and sophomore years of high school and two years of actual IB classes completed your junior and senior years. The program is well recognized among college admission officers and is considered very rigorous and a college-level curriculum. Like AP classes, college credit may be given for certain scores on IB tests. There are even some middle schools that are set up as having IB middle school programs.

Foreign Language

You will need two years minimum of the same foreign language, though some schools might require three years. Highly selective colleges will often want to see four years of foreign language study.

Math

The sequencing of math courses all depends on your starting point in high school and your college major interests. The beginning of this sequence is usually set due to the classes you took in middle school. Pre-algebra and algebra 1 proficiency will not only impact your ability to be successful in algebra 2 and classes requiring algebra 2 as a prerequisite but are also tested on college admission tests (SAT/ACT). Translation: you need to NAIL both your pre-algebra and algebra 1 classes. Plan, at minimum, on having successfully completed algebra 2 by the end of your junior year. If you are interested in business or journalism and your high school offers it, you may find AP statistics more valuable to you than AP calculus AB or BC. If, on the other hand, you are interested in engineering, you definitely want to be taking AP calculus AB or BC to demonstrate your math abilities. As a potential engineering student in college, you will want to have completed a pre-calc class your senior year at minimum.

Also, don't skip math your senior year. Not having math for a year and a half (one academic year and two summers) before starting college means you will be starting college with a somewhat rusty math tool. Keep yourself sharp. If this happens due to a block schedule at your high school, take an online class the summer before you start college to be math sharp for college. Most colleges do require some level of math proficiency to graduate even if you have a non-math intensive major.

Make sure your counselor knows if you are planning on applying for college. There are some math classes that will count for high school graduation but will not be recognized by a college as a college preparatory math class. I would recommend you get in writing from your counselor or math teacher that the class will be recognized by colleges. Taking the easiest math class available may not be the best answer if you want to be college bound. If your counselor doesn't know that you are college bound, they may make a bad recommendation for your senior year schedule. I have had more than one student find out too late that the business math class that they were taking their senior year was not going to be recognized by their dream school as a college preparatory class. It was recognized as a fourth year of high school math but did not meet the requirement for college admissions because the difficulty level was not advanced enough. The four years of math need to get progressively harder. If you consider math to be one of your superpowers, you may want to take two advanced math classes during your senior year or before.

Science

The sequencing of science classes often depends on your interests and the offerings of your high school. If you are interested in medicine as a future major, your high school transcript should show advanced classes in biology (honors or AP), chemistry (honors or AP), and if offered, a class in human anatomy and physiology (honors or AP). Some high schools offer AP environmental science, which also has some advanced biology concepts. Engineering majors should consider taking an advanced physics class, hopefully applied as well as conceptual physics. When you take these classes matters too. At a large public high school in Arizona, advanced students were pushed by counselors and the science department head to go into an honors physics class their freshman year. There were no AP physics offerings at the school.

Those majoring in engineering got a rude awakening when they took a freshman physics class in college, because they had not taken a physics class or reviewed the key equations in over four years. It was almost as if they had never even taken physics. These high-achieving students found themselves struggling just to pass their college freshman year physics class, which was a prerequisite for their major. These were the unintended consequences of their high school curriculum.

English

Usually, English courses are required all four years of high school. Some students will take both AP English language and AP English literature in high school. Some students will take a dual enrollment class as seniors or juniors in high school, which gives them both community college and high school credit for the class. If you are going to an in-state public college and have taken English 101 dual enrollment while in high school, many in-state colleges will give you college credit. It is rarer for out-of-state colleges to give you credit, but they will see the class as elevated rigor over a standard track or honors high school English class.

Social Studies

Requirements for social studies vary widely depending on the state where you live. Common requirements include government, U.S. history, world history, economics (macro or micro). If you think you may want to major in history, politics, international relations, or pre-law, I recommend taking more classes in the social studies arena than what is minimally required for high school graduation.

162

Performing Arts/Visual Arts

Some colleges (specifically, some California colleges) want to see an actual performing art (band, choir, etc.) and may not accept a graphic art class to fulfill this one-year requirement.

Other Requirements

Other possible high school graduation requirements can include passing a basic computer competency class or test, passing a basic keyboarding test, passing a U.S. citizenship test, passing a PE class, or having a certain basic number of high school credits. Private Catholic high schools will often have a certain number of theology classes required. You can find information on basic requirements for graduating from high school either on the high school's or school district's website or by talking to your high school counselor. You should also look at in-state public colleges, or dream colleges if you have any at this point, to see what their requirements are. Some colleges will list two different ranges of classes: those they require and those they recommend. You should always try to complete the number of classes they recommend if you want to be a seriously considered, competitive candidate for admissions. You do need to check the college admission requirements every year, though, because the requirements can change annually.

A Cautionary Tale

If you aren't careful with how you plan your courses, you can run out of time to turn around lagging grades. This is a true story of a student who learned that lesson the hard way. This student had been on the varsity pom squad for three years, was dating the high school quarterback, and came from a family that was financially well-off. She thought she was bigger than her high school and would be going away to college, no sweat. Her mother was her friend who defended her at every turn. If she wanted a fancy Starbucks drink every morning before school, she got it. If she woke up late, her mother called the front office and lied about having a doctor's appointment (at least most of the time). If she didn't turn in an assignment, mom came to the rescue. Sadly, her family ran into some financial troubles her junior year and she had to go without a few things; they had to make their coffee at home, but mom still put it in a Starbucks cup so her daughter could stay "cool." They had to keep up appearances, after all.

When the schoolwork became too difficult, mom said that she didn't have to worry; she would be fine as long as she passed with a D. But things caught up with her. In her senior year, she received notice from her high school that she was in danger of being expelled for unexcused absences in her first period class. Mom had missed calling her in late a few too many times. She had over seven unexcused "tardies" for the semester. Mom was outraged and stormed into the office to turn things around, only to find out that the numbers were not on her side. The high school was at risk of not getting money from the district because of the number of absences her daughter had accumulated. She then found out that, although her daughter was on track to graduate from high school, she was NOT on track to go to college. With a 2.1 GPA, most colleges, including the in-state colleges, did not consider her college ready. She had been doing the minimum required to graduate high school, but not enough to get into in-state colleges.

Some colleges will accept a certain level of test score instead of a certain GPA to get in, but unfortunately there is a relationship between your high school academic skills and your ability to score well on many of those college admissions tests. As an example, a score of 22 on the ACT (with a perfect score being a 36) is considered college ready. This young lady, even with test preparation, was scoring in the 18 to 19 range. She was not ready for a four-year university. We discussed the option of attending the local community college as an alternative to get her ready for the rigors of college, but she was not having it. She wanted to go to a four-year college like all her friends and her boyfriend. On top of everything else, her junior year second semester grades made her academically ineligible to stay on the pom squad. Her mother was distraught...but distraught just a little too late. The daughter started retaking classes online to make up for the Ds that punctuated her transcript, but she was out of runway to get them all done in a year with her proposed senior schedule. Summer can be a great time to retake classes, but she was a senior and her summers were all gone.

The mother also had not gone through the logic that many colleges have January application due dates. That means getting straight As the second semester of senior year to try and turn around a lagging GPA does not work. Admissions decisions are made based on your GPA at the time of application. Yes, you can note on your application that you are retaking classes, but an admissions decision is usually based on what you have done to date, not what you might do in the future. Some colleges have early admissions deadlines in October or November, which means the colleges won't even see the grades from the first semester of your senior year before they make an admissions decision in December. Your student needs to have their act together before the start of their senior year to have the most options for college admission. Now, to compound this young lady's problems, she was only taking four classes per semester her senior year. Unsurprisingly, this was the minimum requirement for her to graduate. That's what all of her "cool" friends were doing, so she felt she should have the same schedule. Well, an immediate "reset" of her schedule required that she take seven classes a day during her senior year both semesters. She found herself as the only senior in freshman-level classes that she was having to retake. Her academic workload was such that many of the parties and get-togethers that seniors attended did not fit into her weekly schedule. She didn't feel so cool anymore, and the "in" crowd had passed her by.

This story does have a semi-happy ending. The in-state college she wanted to attend did have a rolling admissions policy, meaning there was not a hard cutoff for applications in January and they would accept applications as late as June of a student's senior year. She was able, with Herculean effort, to get into a four-year college. She was actually quite smart and faced a motivation hurdle more so than a learning hurdle. She increased her admissions test score to a 22 with ongoing test preparation study and felt certifiably college ready. But many of the "in" crowd moments passed her by during her senior year. The students she had called geeks and nerds were going to amazing, out-of-state, selective universities. They were the new "in" crowd, not the minimum effort group she had been hanging out with.

PARENTAL ALERT: Children will live up to...or down to your expectation of them. Keep the bar high, but within their reach. Your expectations have to be aligned with their true abilities, but if they are attending class, turning in all their homework and assignments and still not doing well on tests and falling short, then you need to assess what could help them. Have them approach the teacher for some additional assignments, instruction, videos, or study suggestions. Have them see the teacher before or after school or at lunch if they are available. If the teacher is still not explaining the material in a way your child understands, then look for peer or professional tutoring to increase mastery of the topics. Let them know what you expect of them in school and let them know you will do everything possible to help them. Reinforce that doing well in school will help them have more options upon graduation. Tell them that the minimum acceptable GPA should be a 3.0 unweighted in academic classes to have a reasonable chance of getting into a four-year university. That wouldn't get them into Stanford or the Ivy League, but it shows that academics is important to them and that they can be successful in college.

PSAT

Your junior year is when your PSAT score counts for National Merit Scholarship purposes and gives you the best idea of how you will actually perform on the SAT. If you are a high-scoring student (meaning your score was over 1250 as a sophomore), then you should prepare to try to knock the ball out of the park on the PSAT in your junior year. Usually, it is given in October. Plan on taking it at school. Your high school will tout the number of National Merit Scholarship candidates they have. Any preparation that you do for your PSAT will apply to taking the SAT, as the tests are similar. The SAT is slightly longer and tests a slightly higher level of math, but the format and general timing is the same. A perfect score on the PSAT is 1520.

College Admissions Testing (ACT and SAT)

This is perhaps the biggest addition to your junior year workload and pressure profile. Yes, many schools have become test optional, but the statistic that students don't know is that at highly selective colleges, approximately 80% of the students that were admitted provided SAT or ACT scores. Also, there is a big difference between test optional and test blind. Test blind colleges will NOT look at scores even if you provide them. Test optional colleges will look at them if provided. Also, test scores are still being used at many colleges for class placement options and scholarships. The trend seems to be towards the test optional model over test blind for most colleges going forward. The exception to that rule, at least during COVID times, is the University of California system and Cal State colleges, as they are committed to being test blind for the time being. Conversely, Florida public colleges require test scores. Rules can change quickly, so a college that is test blind or test optional or requires a test score may not have those same stipulations the following year. Don't just do the minimum when it comes to testing.

Most students perform their college admissions testing during their junior year to strengthen their admissions application or to be more competitive for scholarships. If needed, you may also test at the beginning of your senior year. Many students will take their college admissions test two or three times. Many students test twice during the spring or summer of their junior year and then again the beginning of their senior year, if needed. The reason students might wait until the spring is usually based on their math level.

The first thing you need to determine is which college admissions test is best for you. Having helped thousands of students prepare for these tests, it is with great certainty that I can tell you that each test (SAT and ACT) test different skills in different ways. The SAT predominantly tests critical thinking skills, while the ACT tests analytic skills. At our center, we would often use a student's PSAT score from their junior year and compare it with the score from a practice ACT test to help determine which test is best suited for that student. As a generalization, students who are strong in math and science tend to do better on the ACT, while students who are strong in verbal skills tend to do better on the SAT. However, I always say that you need the data points of at minimum a full recent PSAT and full ACT test to know for sure which one has the higher starting platform. I know of no college that requires both tests, so figuring out which one you are stronger on and focusing your test preparation energies on that test is ideal. There are certainly situations where a student is very strong in reading and writing but struggles so much in math on the SAT that, because the math section is 50% of the overall SAT score, the ACT ends up being the better test for that student. Conversely, there are some aggressive timing constraints on the ACT; I have found that some math and science superstars do better on the SAT because they are able to complete each section and therefore maximize performance. You need to do the work and determine which one is best for YOU and where your biggest opportunity for improvement lies.

> **PARENT ALERT:** Help your student find out which test, the SAT or ACT, is the best test for them. There are many companies like SEC, Kaplan, Barron's, and Princeton Review that will allow you to take both a version of the SAT and ACT test to determine which one is the stronger test for them, free of charge. Do it! Don't spend your child's time and your money preparing for a test that may not be the right one.

Guessing

Both the SAT and the ACT do not penalize for guessing. It is better to have something bubbled in on the test answer sheet than to leave it blank. If you have 10 seconds left on the test (which you will know because you will of course be wearing a watch), you need to mark C…or whatever your favorite guessing letter is…on the remaining questions rather than leaving them blank.

Nature of Content

The ACT, which was designed from high school curriculum, tends to be a very black-and-white test, meaning the content is straightforward. The SAT, on the other hand, was originally created from IQ tests and tends to be much more in the gray area, meaning the questions are more implied, inferred, and nuanced.

Science

The ACT does include a science section of 40 questions that must be completed in 35 minutes. It is not testing specific science knowledge but rather your ability to apply the scientific logical deduction process through reading reports, charts and graphs, exhibits, and raw data. It is the last part of the multiple-choice section of the test, so students are required to complete this section on a brain that can be somewhat fatigued. That being said, many students find this section to be very straightforward. Don't let it intimidate you. You may have to do some extrapolation, but the answers are there in the charts and graphs and the reading.

Math

The math sections are quite different. Both the SAT and ACT test through algebra 2 (the second full year of algebra). You need to make certain that you get as much core algebra 2 knowledge as possible before you test. It should be no surprise that, if you haven't taken algebra 2 yet, you will most likely miss the algebra 2 questions on the test.

The SAT has 58 math questions. There are very, very few, if any, geometry questions. You must read the questions very carefully. You have one hour and 10 minutes to complete the two math sections: 35 minutes for the "no calculator section" and 65 minutes for the calculator section. They are the last two multiple-choice sections of the SAT. There are 20 questions where you are not allowed to use your calculator and 13 questions that are not multiple choice. The non-multiple–choice questions are sections where a student must do the math and write the correct answer on a grid. There is virtually an unlimited number of answer possibilities, including the possibility of fractions and decimals as well as whole numbers to five places. Basically, you have to know the math on these questions as guessing is basically impossible. There are 38 questions in the section where you are allowed to use a calculator. The non-multiple–choice questions are found in both non-calculator and calculator sections of the test.

The ACT has 60 math questions in the second section of the test and you have one hour to complete it. You are allowed to use your calculator throughout the entire math test and all the questions are multiple choice. The ACT does have geometry questions and a couple of questions that broach into trigonometry. To the relief of many, the geometry questions are not proofs.

Reading

There is more reading on the SAT, which includes five passages and 52 questions. There is one fiction passage, two social science passages, and two science passages. There can be two "right" answers in the multiple-choice section, but the SAT wants the best right answer. The ACT has four passages: one fiction, one social science, one nonfiction humanities, and one science. There are 40 questions, 10 per passage. Both contain a dual set of passages that you compare. The biggest difference is in the amount of time given to complete the reading section, which is the first section on the SAT and the third section on the ACT. The ACT allows

35 minutes to complete the reading section while the SAT allows one hour and five minutes. In either section, underlining and annotating the passages can be VERY helpful.

Writing

Both tests focus on two major areas of writing: (1) grammar skills and (2) editing skills. There are 75 English questions in the first section on the ACT, and you have 45 minutes to complete it. There are 48 questions in the second section on the SAT, and you have 50 minutes to complete it.

Essay

The essay section of the test is optional for the ACT. The SAT no longer offers an essay section. Whether or not it is truly optional on the ACT, however, depends on the requirements of the schools to which you are applying. Not all colleges use the score on the essay section for admissions considerations, but some do. Again, you can go to the website of the college you are applying to in order to determine if you need to take the essay section.

If you will be writing the essay on test day, it will be completed at the very end of the test after the multiple-choice sections. The ACT essay is a persuasive essay that wants you to choose a perspective on the prompt, which is usually some kind of moral, ethical, or social dilemma often pertinent to high school students. You have 40 minutes. The essays are handwritten, and spelling and grammar DO count. You will undoubtedly be writing quickly, but if the essay is illegible, it cannot score well.

This writing section on the test is not the same thing as the essay required on the Common Application or in the writing supplement section of your application (if required by your college). And this brings us to the topic of writing skills. If you have ignored English and writing throughout your academic career, there is no possible way to score well on these essays. By the time you are a junior, it is extremely difficult to improve your writing skills in a few weeks. I have worked with students on college admissions essays that are full of almost unreadable run-on sentences, middle school grammar mistakes, and elementary-level four-letter words (good, nice, kind). The time to pay serious attention to writing skills is at least your freshman year.

Practical Tips

For both the SAT and ACT, here are some basic tips:

- Bring multiple pencils.
- Bring two fully charged calculators or one calculator and extra batteries. You are not allowed to use your phone as a calculator. Check the testing websites for a list of acceptable calculators: www.collegeboard.com (SAT) or www.act.org (ACT). Generally, the testing agencies don't want you to have calculators that can store data or take pictures or record formulas.
- Dress in layers and pack a jacket.
- Sleep well the week before and the night before the test.
- Make sure you have your picture IDs and test admissions ticket.
- Make sure you know how to get to your testing location, with alternate routes calculated as well.
- Get there 15 minutes early and know where to park.

- Wear a watch. Many testing rooms do not have clocks in them and even if they do, they may be behind you. Make sure your watch can't store data, take pictures, or record information, as they will not be allowed in the testing room. Also make certain it doesn't tick loudly, as to not disturb other test takers.

- DO NOT TAKE YOUR PHONE INTO THE TESTING SITE. There are so many horror stories about students who have had their test invalidated because they had their phones in the vicinity of the test. One student had completed her test, and when the proctor picked up her test, she reached into her purse and got out her phone to call her mother for a ride. Unfortunately, there were still tests on other students' desks. The proctor pulled her test and told her it was being cancelled. Another student had taken his phone out in the bathroom at the break when a proctor walked in. The proctor took the young man back to the testing room, pulled his test, and invalidated it. It's best to avoid the temptation and just leave your phone either in your car or at home. The reason they are so strict is to make sure that the tests are not compromised or leaked in any way. Because tests are given in multiple time zones on the same day, they do not want tests or questions or answers floating around in advance. Truthfully, you don't either.

Lead and Create

Hopefully by now you have started to find your interests and have some ideas about what activities you truly enjoy and feel enriched by. Now is the time to step into leadership shoes and start highlighting this area on your resume. Many college admissions officers highly prize leadership. It can DEMONSTRATE that a student knows who they are and, as the saying goes, can not only walk on water but can freeze it so others can walk with them. I often hear the lament from students that all the leadership positions at the established clubs at their high schools "are already full" (which I don't totally believe). In any case, what is preventing that student from starting their own club or organization in an area that interests them? CREATE something new. Participate in the community in a meaningful way. Lead a group to raise money for a disease that may have affected their family, such as cancer, Alzheimer's, or diabetes. Fundraising walks abound in most communities, so start a club on campus that participates in raising money for that cause. Faith-based organizations often have opportunities for teens. Find your cause and lead. Ideally, have that leadership opportunity make sense with your interests and future pursuits. There are many organizations that build teen leadership skills. Some of the organizations that are very strong in that area in most greater metropolitan areas are: National Charity League, Boys and Girls Club, Boys Team Charity, Project C.U.R.E., the Mayor's Youth Council, Boys and Girls State, Junior Civil Air Patrol, science centers, art museums, and Miracle League. Each local community will have its own list of outside community leadership-building groups.

NCAA Clearinghouse

If you are a serious athlete who is hoping to play in college, it is a good idea to check NCAA requirements early on in your junior year to make certain you are on track academically to be eligible to be recruited and play in college. NCAA has some hardline rules on GPA and test requirements in high school. One requirement has been that a student complete high school in four years. You will also need to have your test scores and transcripts sent to NCAA to verify that you are eligible. They have their own code, just like the individual colleges do, that can be found on the website for CollegeBoard, ACT, or Naviance/Parchment/ whatever transcript service your high school uses.

What Do You Want? Checklist

Now is also the time to start really defining what you are looking for in a college. One of the first things you need to see eye to eye with your parents is the financial situation of your family. You need to talk about what is "doable" for college in terms of your parents' participation in paying for your tuition, room and board, books, phone, computer, etc. Your parents need to be realistic with you so you both understand the parameters. Will you need to get a part-time job? Will you be able to have a car (if the campus even allows freshmen to have cars)? Will you need to live at home? If finances are a concern (and when are they not), be aware that many colleges do offer some form of financial aid or grants. It is important to research your top priority schools and determine a financing plan. Other things to consider are:

- Proximity to home
- Size of town: urban, rural, college town, suburban
- Environment: coast, mountains, lakes, winter sports, four seasons
- Weather: snow, humidity, temperature

- Size of college: small, medium, large
- Housing options: on campus, off campus, commuter campus, single rooms, shared bathrooms
- Academic offerings (very important): majors, ROTC, study abroad, internships (very important), research projects, theological studies, student-to-teacher ratios
- Average number of years it takes a student to graduate
- Activities: Greek life, intramural sports, NCAA sports, clubs on campus, robust theatre program, band, orchestra, religious clubs, LGBTQ+ club, dance program, school newspaper or journal
- Services: career counseling (very important), financial aid counseling, health services, ESL, tutoring support centers, ADD/ADHD support

Letters of Recommendation

In recent years, students have more often started asking teachers for letters of recommendation at the end of their junior year. Generally, colleges want to see three letters of recommendation with one being from your high school counselor and two from teachers you have had your junior or senior year in a core academic class like English, math, science, social studies, or foreign language. Colleges that have de-emphasized test scores may ask for more letters of recommendation and allow additional sources such as a coach, music teacher, employer, faith-based organization, or community service director. It varies by college. If the college allows additional letters, I recommend the students provide them. It generally means that the college highly values the letters as input for their decision process. It allows you to give the college more insight into who you are and the depth of your character and leadership skills.

College Visits

You should continue your college visiting schedule and visit at least three colleges this year.

Three colleges I will visit this year:

1.

2.

3.

CHAPTER 6

SENIOR YEAR

PARENT ALERT: Don't assume the rules and process you went through in high school are the same for your student. It is a VERY different academic world out there. Be willing to listen and learn with your child. (Reading this book is a great step!)

Grades Still Count

Although many colleges have application due dates before you may even have your first semester senior year grades, they do ask what classes you will be enrolled in and will know the difficulty of your senior schedule. Many high schools offer students the option of doing half or abbreviated schedules their senior years, and students who don't need to retake a class where they may have received a C, D, or F are often eligible for those schedules. Usually, I recommend that students take advantage of that option ONLY if they have something very, very important that they will be doing in their spare time. That doesn't mean filling out college applications, because most of your classmates will be doing that. If you have an opportunity to do something unique with that time, it could be a good idea to take advantage of that alternate schedule. Examples of unique opportunities might include: becoming part of a research project, starting an amazing community service project, taking advantage of an amazing job opportunity, learning a special skill not offered at your school, raising a substantial amount of money for a charity, starting your own business, or taking a class at your local community college. Otherwise, you should plan on having a regular course schedule. You are not done yet—don't stop growing in your senior year!

> **PARENT ALERT:** Your student still has to graduate from high school. Don't let them lose steam. Senioritis can be a real thing. Make sure your student knows, however, that in your house, "senioritis is not allowed."

Retest

If needed, you can still take the SAT or ACT the beginning of your senior year and get the score back in time for your application deadlines. Some colleges, like the University of Arizona, will allow you to take a test up until early spring to qualify for greater scholarship consideration. Also, colleges with rolling admissions may allow later test dates. Generally, the recommendation is to take the test again early in your senior year. Since every college differs in terms of their last testing dates for admission, to be safe, I would say don't wait until later than October to take the test again.

College Application Deadlines

Get ahead of your applications, and don't wait until the last minute. Every school sets their own admissions deadline, and those could change. Some colleges, like the University of Alabama, Ole Miss, and the University of Arizona, actually open their applications in July. The "big" application sites like Common Application and Coalition Application open on August 1st. Currently, the University of California system has a smaller window for application submission, which is only open from October 1st through November 30th. University of Southern California has a scholarship application deadline on December 1st while their admissions application is January 15th. You will need to check the individual colleges' websites to know what deadline dates are for your year, both for scholarships and admissions. What may have been true for an older sibling or friend may not be true for your particular year and schools.

PARENT ALERT: Your child needs to spend some time during the summer before their senior year researching where they want to go and knowing key due dates for EACH college. You should also know the dates as they have financial consequences. Have a weekly or biweekly sit-down with your child to review the status of financial and application deadlines and what schools are still on their radar. My experience is that the list can change dramatically during the senior year.

The Essay

Although your GPA in rigorous classes is the most important element in the application review process, other important components of your application that are evaluated include test scores, letters of recommendation, and essay(s). The essay differentiates you from other students. Generally, it is not something that is written in one sitting. The thinking time before writing usually takes three times as long as the actual writing. Your essay needs to be reflective, demonstrate knowledge, have great voice, and be personal and genuine. It needs to tell the director of admissions something about you that is not obvious from any other part of the application. It needs to be an essay that only you could have written.

One of the pitfalls many students fall into is making statements that are so general that anyone could have written them. An example would be, "I want to help people." That is a wonderful sentiment to convey and quality to possess, but it needs to be personalized. "I spent last summer driving over 500 miles delivering water bottles to homeless individuals in Phoenix, Arizona" says the same thing but in a very personal way. I worked with one student who wanted to convey the sentiment that he loved the outdoors. Rather than starting his essay with that sentence, he chose to open with, "Last year, I slept over 100 nights in a tent above 5,000 feet." It communicates the same thing but in a personal way that captures the reader's attention. The essay prompts are essentially asking, "who are you?" Highly prized characteristics that directors of admissions often look for are demonstrations of character, resilience, compassion, and diversity. In Part Two, we will talk about how to help you answer the heart of this question.

The Interview

Interview prep is my favorite thing to do with my students. More colleges and universities do not offer interviews than do. However, there are places where the interview is very important, such as the military service academies, MIT, and Ivy League universities. College interviews can be one of the more anxiety-inducing parts of the college admissions process for students. Overall, it may only account for about 5 to 10% of the overall admissions review but it does become more important if conducted by an on-campus admissions officer.

If you are applying to schools where an interview may be part of the process, let me just give you a few things to think about:

- The interview is an opportunity to give dimension to your application. It should be viewed as a way to give spice and color to your application and to make you memorable.
- It is a conversation, not an inquisition. There really is no right or wrong answer unless your answer is not a genuine representation of yourself. Since it is a two-way conversation, you will be given a chance at the end to ask questions of the interviewer, and you should.
- Interviews are frequently conducted with the college's alumni who live in your area. Generally, the interviewers in that setting are not gatekeepers, but they can give their impressions and insights about you to the directors of admissions.
- The potential questions that will be asked are as varied as the interviewers. They usually try and match the alumni

with the interest areas of the student, if at all possible. You need to research your interviewer before you meet them. Professional networking sites like LinkedIn can provide helpful information about their background and give you some ideas for questions to ask at the end of the interview.

Possible interview questions include:

"Tell me about yourself." This is by far the hardest question you will be asked, and it is generally the first question asked. Most students fumble this answer. It sounds like a softball question, but if you haven't thought about it in advance, it is almost impossible to improvise an eloquent response. I am not recommending that you memorize your answer, but I am recommending that you practice answering that question out loud, either while looking in the mirror or having your parents ask you that question a few times (especially in the car as you are headed to the interview). You are the expert on this subject. You need to assume they know nothing about you and tell them the four or five most important things they need to know. I usually recommend you talk about your academics, your passion, your leadership in community service or school activities, your most prized awards, what you want to major in, and something about your work or family life. Remember, if you don't tell them, they are not going to know. I find students to be exceptionally modest when asked this question, so don't be afraid to talk about your unique strengths (your weirdness!). Your answer should be longer than 30 seconds, and make sure you look the interviewer in the eye and speak up.

"Why do you want to go to our school?" Have a specific reason ready. Look through the major you are interested in on the college's

website and find a class that you would want to take. Find a support organization for that major that you could see yourself joining. Find a research project on campus that you would want to take part in. Find a foreign campus that you would like to go to while there. Find an aspect of the college's curriculum that is unique and interesting to you (e.g., the ability to double major or have a specific emphasis area). Find clubs or activities that you would like to join. Find an internship opportunity that is interesting to you. Have a real answer, not: "I have a friend who is applying here" or "The campus is close to the ocean" or "I like the weather there" (those are all actual answers I have heard from students, by the way).

"What do you plan on majoring in?" No, you will not be handcuffed to your answer. Some students really don't know, and that is okay because most colleges don't require you to declare your major until the end of sophomore year. Even if you are not sure what you want to major in, be ready to talk about a few areas of interest and why you are interested in them.

"Why should our school accept you?" Be prepared to match the college's stated pillars to your story. First, you have to know what those pillars are, which are usually pretty easy to find on the website. Put yourself in the position of a director of admissions. Why should they let you in? Do you fit their academic profile? How are you going to add to their community? Draw a picture in the interviewer's mind of how you are going to be active and involved on the campus. What special skills or attributes or talents or characteristics or unique perspectives might you be bringing to the campus population?

"What do you know about our school?" Be specific about academic strengths, campus size, admission stats, notable programs, or alumni, and why it is the best fit for you.

"What are your academic strengths?" This could be subjects or skills, like organization, critical thinking, analytic thinking, planning, efficiency, or multitasking. Be ready to give an example of why it is a strength.

"What are your academic weaknesses?" Are you a perfectionist? Do you want to take all the classes? Do you like to go extra deep in all your studies? Do you tend to ask too many questions?

"What are you looking forward to the most at our school?" This is another instance where you need to have really done your research before your interview on what that school has to offer and relate it to your demonstrated high school experience.

"Where do you see yourself being in the next 5 or 10 years?" Make sure you think BOLD with your answer. Of course, graduating from "My Dream College" must be on the list.

"What is your dream job?" Again, think BOLD. Visualize where you will be in life when you are 65 years old. What do you want to have accomplished? Have you won specific awards? Written a book? Earned a doctorate degree? Founded a charity? What will you have done to get that dream job?

"Do you have a favorite book?" I always asked this question when I was interviewing high school students for jobs at our business. Stick to high school–worthy books, though. I have gotten

answers of *Diary of a Wimpy Kid* and *Goodnight Moon*, which wasn't exactly what I was hoping for in an answer.

"What is the most important thing going on in the world today?" I have seen this question being asked frequently by highly selective and elite colleges. Hopefully, you will have been reading newspapers, listening to TED Talks, or visiting media sites that can help you formulate an answer. Talk with your parents about this topic as well because some of the world happenings may have a direct impact on your family. What is going on that may impact those things that you care about?

"Do you have any questions for me?" Yes, you do…at least three. You can ask about the direction of the college over the next five years, the interviewer's experience at the college, whether they would have done anything differently while there, if they have any advice for you about the admissions process, or how graduating from that school has affected their career. There is also the "killer" closing question that a few of my most confident students have used, but it is one that must be phrased very succinctly and with a direct stare into the interviewer's eyes: "Do you have any concerns about my ability to be successful at this school"? And then…listen closely. If they do identify any concerns, directly address them. For example, if your GPA is a little low, explain how your freshman year was a transitional year but you have improved tremendously in your more rigorous junior year classes, which are a better representation of how you will do at the college level. If they don't identify any concerns, then you leave the room or coffee shop knowing you have done a great job at representing yourself. If you feel comfortable asking this question and potentially responding to any concerns, this closing

question can go a long way in helping you nail the interview. And, of course, you will send a personal thank you note within 48 hours.

The Gap Year

Gap years can be a great option for some students, and there are a variety of reasons why a student might consider it. Some students use gap years to earn money to help pay for college or take care of family. Other students just aren't emotionally ready or may be particularly young and their parents want to wait until they are legally adults before sending them off to college. There are many gap year programs out there that provide a range of experiences, from research or journalism to language immersion or music. If you think you are a competitive applicant and believe you can gain an acceptance letter to your dream school, it might be better to first get the acceptance letter and then defer attending for one year. If you are taking a gap year to try to become more competitive for college, then you want to start researching what might be available for you the summer in between your junior and senior years.

There are a couple of considerations when deciding whether to take a gap year. The first one is cost. Gap year programs can be expensive, so you need to weigh that against the cost of going to college out of high school. Second, if you are thinking of majoring in certain subjects in college, then taking a year off may present some challenges. For example, if you plan on majoring in a foreign language, math, or engineering, those subjects require specific skills in order to be ready to start college-level work. If you aren't using those skills for a year and a summer, it will make that first quarter of Mandarin, calculus, or differential equations much harder than if you had gone straight from a high school class.

Finding the Right Fit

One of the most important steps in the college application process is finding schools that are the right fit for you. Think through all the factors involved with choosing a school and create a list of top 10 "need to have" requirements. Ideally, this process starts in your freshman year and, by the end of your junior year, you have a notebook or spreadsheet with all of your notes and a "Top 10" list. But, even if you start this process during your senior year, it isn't too late. Here are some factors to help you better define your dream school.

Academic Offerings

First of all, does the school offer the major(s) you are or might be interested in? Do you need or want an ROTC program? Are you hoping to attend a foreign campus, maybe even in a particular part of the world? Can you earn your teaching certification or pilot's license? Do they have a direct admit nursing program? Do they offer interesting internships and have relationships with local businesses? Are research opportunities available? How well do students perform on graduate school standardized tests (like the MCAT, LSAT, GMAT, or GRE)?

Some colleges offer unique programming, such as Semester at Sea, study abroad, and exchanges with other American schools.

Brown University students can apply to take classes at the Rhode Island School of Design, Columbia University students can audition to take classes at Julliard, and students at Barnard can also take classes at Columbia University. Some schools have excellent support programs for students who have diagnosed learning disabilities like the SALT (Strategic Alternative Learning Techniques) program at the University of Arizona, which supports students who have learning and attention difficulties. Marist College has a similar learning support program.

For many students, the availability of an honors program can be enticing. Depending on the college, honors programs can have perks like smaller class sizes, prioritized registration in classes, unique course offerings, and special consideration for research assignments, foreign campus opportunities, internships, and scholarships.

School Type

There is a wide variety of college types. There are two-year colleges that end in a certificate or associate's degree and four-year schools where you graduate with a bachelor's degree. Some schools also have graduate studies programs. Schools can offer liberal arts, technical, art, or music education. There are men's colleges and women's colleges, historically Black colleges and universities, and religious-based schools.

If you have no idea what you want to major in, then you want to go to a college that will have a lot of different major options. If you want to major in engineering, then a pure liberal arts college may not be the best fit for you. Conversely, if you want to major in philosophy, a technical college may not be the best place to be for you.

School Size

This can be a big deal. A small college can be smaller than some high schools. A small college would have fewer than 5,000 students, a medium college may have 5,000 to 15,000 students, and a large college could have over 15,000 students. There are also mega-colleges like the University of Central Florida, Texas A&M, Arizona State University, and Penn State that have over 40,000 undergraduates on campus. If you went to a very small high school, jumping to a mega-large university could be difficult. Visit the campus to get a better sense of your comfort levels. Another thing to look at is the undergraduate-to-graduate student ratio. If there are more grad students than undergrad, the resource allocation may not be favorable to undergrads.

Religious Affiliation

Many colleges keep track of statistics that deal with the religious affiliation of their students. I have worked with students who needed there to be a strong Jewish representation within the college and another set of students who wanted to make sure that they could attend Catholic mass on or near campus. They said it was important to them to quickly find a subset of the college that they felt they could relate to and most likely had similar values or upbringing to theirs.

Proximity to home

Do you want to be able to come home seven days a week, one day a week, one day a month, once a semester, once a year, for the holidays, or for the summer? If you want to go far from home, then you and your parents just need to discuss what that means. Some families refine their college list to schools only within a certain number of miles or travel hours from key family members (grandparents, aunts, uncles, cousins, etc.).

Environment

Do you want to live in a big city, suburb, or college town? Do you prefer East Coast, West Coast, the South, or the Midwest?

Geography

Do you want to be near the beach or ski slopes? Do you need access to lakes or forests? Are mountain air and green trees a must, or do you prefer the buzz of a city that never sleeps?

Temperature

Can you handle humidity or dry heat over 100 degrees? Do you need snow or sunshine or are you happiest in the rain? Do you like having four seasons or a temperate climate that stays the same year-round?

Class Size

At many schools, college freshmen will inevitably be in those large, auditorium-sized classes. Many schools keep statistics on average class sizes. It's no surprise that, the bigger the college, the bigger the class sizes can be in the first two years. At smaller schools, however, you might be in class sizes that are more similar to your high school class size.

Athletics and Academic Comfort

If you are planning to be a college athlete, review the school's GPA and test score averages. I have seen some very talented athletes get into colleges where they are below the 25th percentile of admitted students and end up becoming ineligible to play because of NCAA rules about academic performance. Usually there are extra tutoring resources available to college varsity athletes and the few well-known "easy" classes for them to attend. But, if for some reason they are unable to continue playing sports due to an injury or academic workload, they need to know that they will still be happy at the college they have chosen.

Outside of Academics

Do you hope to sit in the stands in the fall watching a football game, or are there certain sports you want your college to have? Do you want your school to have a strong band, dance, or theater program? Would you want to join a sorority or fraternity? What are your preferences for housing (on campus, off campus, commuter)? Do you have special dietary needs that would have to be addressed? Are you looking for special cultural experience opportunities (e.g., The French House)? Have you been involved with community work that you want to continue in college? What clubs would you be interested in joining? Even though you may not be majoring in art, is there an art department so you can continue to grow your graphic art skills? Is there a college literary magazine or newspaper that you could write for or a radio or TV center where you could get involved? Does the school have an LGBTQ+ center or group? Is there a faith-based organization? Church/Mosque/Synagogue/Faith-based organization center?

Financials

Review cost options and know the difference in costs for the various options.

Class Credit

Check to see what level of credit you might be able to have as you enter your freshman year at the college. Many schools offer college credit for certain types of classes you take in high school, and that information is typically on their website. For example, they may offer credit for freshman English or English 101 at the college level if a student has completed a class and AP test at a certain level. Some colleges will give credit for passing with a 3, while others will require a 4 or 5 to give credit. The same can be said for IB or community college classes. Some students may be able to complete college in three years or less depending on how much credit they receive while still in high school. This can directly affect the cost of college. Oftentimes, community college credit will be carried onto the same state's university or college. It can be a little more difficult trying to transfer the credit to a state university in another state or to a private college.

Matriculation (graduation) rates

A statistic that may be a little harder to find but is also important in the context of cost is matriculation rates. The statistics that a lot of colleges keep now are on six-year matriculation, not four. In fact, the four-year matriculation rate at public colleges and universities is 33.3% while the six-year rate is 57.5%. At private colleges and universities, the four-year graduation rate is 52.8%, and 65.4% (U.S. Department of Education) earn a degree in six years. Be aware that a college with a long matriculation rate may end up costing you a lot more to get your degree.

> **PARENT ALERT:** Help your child define what they are looking for in a college experience. Creating a list of what they really want will help them match their needs with the offerings of the colleges. Sometimes they will find that their "dream college" in reality has none of the attributes of the kind of college experience they are looking for. And sometimes your idea of the best college experience may not fit with what they want for the next four years of their lives. It can be tempting to want our children to follow in our footsteps, but it's important that they find their own path that fits their unique personality and goals.

Deciding on a Major

One important way to take the lead is to figure out your major. If you still aren't sure what you want to major in, be proactive about working through that process.

- Explore interests during summer(s)
- Read *What Color Is Your Parachute?* or *Who Moved My Cheese?*
- Take the Myers-Briggs personality test (you can find a free version online)
- Sit in your room, look around, and reflect on what you surround yourself with and why
- Answer the question: "What are you passionate about?"
- Review what you spend most of your time doing and try new things

What if the college you choose ends up not being the right college? Well, if you throw a wide net in terms of the level of colleges that you are applying to, you should get in somewhere. If you did your homework and research on the college, it certainly increases the chance that you will go to the "right" college, and there may be more than one "right" college. You can always try to transfer colleges, though this is a little harder to do as many colleges' transfer student acceptance rate is even lower than their overall acceptance rate. If you decide to change your major, you are in good company as about 50% of all students change their major by their junior year. Although colleges ask what you plan on majoring in, they do not handcuff you to it. Many colleges don't require you to actually declare your major until the end of your sophomore year in college. If you start down one track your freshman year and decide to change at the beginning of your junior year, it may take you a little longer to graduate but you are not forced to finish a major that does not work for you. Personally, I started out as an international relations major with an emphasis in Economics, and although I completed the requirements for the major, I ended up getting my degree in communications journalism. The writer in me won out.

Top 10 Tips for College Applications

1. Spell check

I once worked with an impressive student who was the senior class president of a large high school, participated in the most rigorous academic program available at his high school, and was going to graduate with an International Baccalaureate Certification. He had his eyes set on the highly competitive Barrett Honors program at Arizona State University, one of the top five honors programs in the country. His mother asked me to review his essay; she knew his superpower was math and not writing. I thought to myself, "He's an IB student for goodness' sake. Surely, he knows how to write. Why would he need anyone else to review his essay?" Reluctantly, he agreed to let me review his essay. And I am glad I did, because he had committed a critical error that would have guaranteed to get him denied admission to the elite program despite having stellar qualifications otherwise. First, when I met with him, I read the essay to him out loud. It's amazing how many errors can be found when a person who has not written the essay reads it out loud to you. With that process, we made several clarifications, fixed grammatical errors, and changed a few prepositions and word choices. But, the biggest problem was one spelling mistake that spell check had not picked up: the name of the honors program. He had misspelled the word Barrett, writing "Barett" with one "r" in several instances. Why would you admit a student who hadn't taken the time to know how to spell the very program they were applying to? We caught it and changed it. He applied early through their priority application process and was accepted, but I know the outcome would have been very different if he hadn't let someone else review his essay.

Get help from someone before submitting your essay, whether it's an independent college consultant (ICC), college admissions coach, English teacher, or a school counselor. Family members, such as parents, siblings, or grandparents, can be helpful, though family reviews can be a little tricky depending on your relationship with them and how much they know about the college application process. On the other hand, they may have valuable insights into who you are or things about yourself that you may be underestimating.

2. Don't repeat yourself

The idea of the essay is to give the directors of admissions a better sense of who you are, not to repeat things they already know about you. One example might be an elite athlete writing their essay about a particular sport, because this may not necessarily tell them things they don't already know about you. The fact that the applicant is an elite athlete tells the admission committee that they are capable of multi-processing, are competitive, value being part of a team, and work hard. That student would want to focus on another aspect of who they are in their essay, such as something about their family or unique interests.

3. *Read and follow directions*

If the directions for the application essay says 650 words or less, then make sure it is 650 words or less. Titles, if you have one for your essay, do count in the word count. I also recommend trying to get just under the number (e.g., 600 words to 650 words). It is an extremely difficult task to explain to someone who you are in 650 words, and I feel it is almost impossible to do it in a lot less than that. Certainly, don't be lazy with minimal effort. But, with word count, make sure that the first thing the directors of admissions know about you is that you can follow directions.

4. *Read the word "recommended" as "required"*

Do a complete and thorough job of completing your application, which includes not skipping optional essays. If there is an optional essay, it is just an opportunity for you to tell the admissions department more about you. If you have the "option" of providing additional letters of recommendation and can find solid recommendations from sources that the college will accept, then take the extra step and provide them. The individual college applications will tell you whether or not they will accept additional letters. Make sure they are good recommendations, however. Better to have three good recommendations than three good ones and one bad one.

5. *Don't wait until the last minute to hit submit*

Several years ago on November 30th, the entire admissions website for the University of California went down on the last day to submit an application. UC was gracious and extended the application due date, but students were not sure if their applications had gone through. Some even had to reenter their entire application. Try to hit submit a few days before the deadline date to avoid any issues: websites being down, internet being down, power outages, the zombie apocalypse, etc. It is a stressful enough time...don't add to your stress quotient by waiting until the last minute. Ask your parent for help with making a plan to stay ahead of the deadlines, including an Excel spreadsheet if need be.

6. Check college requirements

Make certain you know what the minimum high school academic requirements are for each college you are applying to. The colleges will list on their websites what their minimum class requirements are and what they prefer to see. Many colleges only require two years of the same foreign language, but some do require three and many highly selective colleges will prefer four. The same can be said for science requirements. In addition, some departments within the college may have higher GPA/test score/class level requirements than just general admission to the college. Doing the minimum needed to graduate from high school does not mean you have done what is needed to get into college.

7. Keep your story consistent

Hopefully in the telling of your story there is consistency, meaning a thread that can be pulled through the entire application and tells a story that makes sense. As an example, if you are telling the college that you are interested in a bio or pre-med major with the goal of becoming a doctor, then it would make sense to see related activities on your application: volunteering at a hospital, internship or shadowing with a doctor, first aid and CPR training, participation in a research project, planning a blood drive, or starting a medical club. Those activities make sense to your story. Maybe you also take extra honors, AP, or dual enrollment classes in math or science or you take extra classes after school at your community college or during the summer at a college that you hope to attend. Your application should reflect that you are DOING things that demonstrate your interests and that make sense together. If you are telling a college that you want to major in communications or journalism, then it would make sense that you are involved in writing for your school's newspaper or literary magazine, or starting a newspaper or magazine at your high school if they don't have one, entering writing contests, writing blogs, submitting work to a local community newsletter or local newspaper, and taking additional high-level writing classes at your high school or at a college in the summer. Demonstrate that you love to write. Your story needs to be true to who you are and what you want to become.

8. Take the lead

Pretty soon, you will be on your own. It will be up to you to get good grades, take care of yourself, and become independent. You need to be interested in college because you understand all the advantages you will have by exploring a higher education. Of course, you will have guidance and encouragement from other people in your life, namely your parents, but ultimately you are the one who must take the lead.

9. Show depth

Once you have identified what you are interested in pursuing, dive deep. If you are looking for admission to a highly selective college, becoming "world class" in something—deep, expert, professional, championed, nationally recognized—is something that you will be evaluated on. They won't just look at how smart and busy you are or whether you are a leader and involved in the community. Your interest has to be deep and intense and focused. This is one of the BIGGEST issues that I see in students' applications.

10. Don't underestimate yourself

In putting together resumes and filling out applications, students tend to be more humble than bold. One young lady I worked with had a very difficult time coming up with the topic for her application essay. The characteristic that we had chosen to highlight was her compassion. She was at the top of her class at a prestigious Catholic girl's high school in the greater Phoenix area. She had started a nonprofit organization where she collected tennis shoes for children in Tibet after going on an outreach trip with her school. The day before she left, she played soccer with some of the children in the village where her group was staying. They were younger but delighted in playing the game. However, she was shocked to see them playing on the rocky soccer field with bare feet. When she got back to her room, her collection of Nike and Adidas shoes seemed out of place. They had NO shoes and she had brought five different pairs just for her two-week trip. She left all her shoes behind for the villagers and began a shoe drive at her school. Over two years, she helped collect hundreds of pairs of new shoes for the village. The small detail she had "forgotten" to mention in her essay was that she had traveled back to Tibet twice to physically deliver the shoes with money she had raised herself for the trip and had met with the Dalai Lama in the Forbidden City of Lhasa on both occasions. Most people in their lifetime do not get to meet the Dalai Lama, and certainly not twice. That's quite an opening line in a college application essay. I had to pull that information out of her, though, because she didn't think it was important. I will never forget the call I received from her in the early spring when she told me that she had been accepted to her dream school…I actually think she may have been dancing around her living room when she called.

Parents, How to Avoid Common Mistakes During the College Application Process

Talk with your child about financial parameters for college

This is a very important conversation to have. Are you expecting them to contribute a certain amount through scholarships? Will they be expected to hold down a job while in college? Are they expected to maintain a certain GPA while in college to receive funding from you? Will they be expected to contribute a certain amount of money each summer? Will they be expected to take out loans? If so, how much? Merit money is very different than need-based financial aid. Need-based financial aid usually starts with the parent filling out the FAFSA (Free Application for Federal Student Aid). This will be your job. Your student needs to be an active participant in this process, though, if a scholarship is needed. Financial situations can greatly affect where your student may decide to apply to college. You don't want to stress them out about your financial situation, but they do need to be aware of what is and is not possible. Our daughters did have some responsibilities to help pay for college (approximately 10% of the overall cost of their college educations), which meant they had some skin in the game. You need to have the conversation.

One important thing to be aware of as a parent is the average number of years it takes a student to graduate and the average graduation rate at each school. At many colleges, students graduate in five or six years. Nationwide, the number of students who graduate from public colleges in four years is 33%; for private colleges, it is 53%. Some of that is due to students changing majors, not being able to get into the classes they need to graduate, or personal family situations, but unfortunately that number has been declining over the years, not increasing. Some of the decline has to do with how the number is now calculated to be more inclusive of all students, such as nontraditional students and students who are parents or have full-time jobs. Still, it is a shocking statistic. This is something to investigate before you send in that first tuition check. Both you and your child should do that research before attending. If you can't find the number on the college's website, you can write an email to the admissions department and ask.

DO NOT...repeat...DO NOT write the application essay for them

I can't tell you how many times I have read application essays that were written by parents. It's obvious when a parent has written an essay. The voice is different. The language is different. The tone is different. The examples used are different. The references are different. The vocabulary is different. Directors of admissions can tell too. Genuine voice is critical. The reflection needs to be their reflection…their epiphany. Yes, you should read their essay (with their permission), but don't edit it to the point of rewriting it. Make sure they get help from someone in the crafting of telling their story. Talk with them about being reflective and ask what they are thinking about writing. Help them remember who they are. But let them write it.

Keep updated on timeliness but resist helicoptering

"Trust but verify." This is where the weekly or biweekly meeting comes in. They need to be driving the action, but you need to be updated on progress. They may need help, and this is their opportunity to ask for it. Very soon, they will be in charge of their own trajectory. Help them learn how to project manage, including deadlines, while still having them start taking charge. Students who can't handle this may not be ready to go to a four-year college.

Help them visit colleges and define what they need

Virtual college visits are becoming more prevalent, but whether the college visit is in person or virtual, make sure you go with them. Make them define for you what it is that they like or don't like about any college trip. Have them take notes on each visit because it is very easy to confuse which college was which. When they are exploring school websites, make sure they record average admission statistics and research the department that they are interested in majoring in. Have them look at foreign campuses they might be interested in attending, research projects they might be interested in participating in, clubs on campus that appeal to them, special programs that make that college compelling (e.g., Semester at Sea), and which classes and professors they are excited about. They need to RESEARCH, RESEARCH, RESEARCH! Before physically visiting a school, they should know the answers to all of those questions.

Help them see themselves as others see them

Over the years of working with thousands of high school students, I have only worked with three who I would put in the "offensively and undeservedly braggartly" category. The large majority of students have been in the "humble" category. Some of them are still struggling a little with who they are or who they have become. I have frequently had to say to students, "Show the school who you are. If you don't tell them, they are not going to know. Often, they don't get to meet you face-to-face, so you have to *show* them who you are." In the next part of the book, I will share several exercises to help them see who they have become.

Help them remember that they are more than just a GPA and test score

Yes, GPA and test scores are very important elements of the college admissions review. But, it is not the ONLY thing that many colleges look at. College admissions directors need to make sure that the students they admit can be academically successful, but many colleges do "holistic" reviews, meaning they evaluate other elements they feel are important for their student communities.

These include leadership, community participation, passion, athletic talents, performing arts abilities, ethnicity, income levels, and cultural background. This is about being their biggest fan. Make them apply to some "stretch" colleges. Help them remember all the other important, wonderful things about themselves during this time of self-doubt, possible rejection, and self-reflection.

Don't forget to breathe

Don't project your fears onto them. Believe me, they have enough of their own. I have had several students break down and cry in my office during college application time. I have had even more parents break down with the fear that their child's dreams won't be realized. At this point in the process, they don't need to carry any more fear than they are carrying on their own. They need help and support and encouragement and reality. I have seen students get analysis paralysis where they are so afraid of making a mistake with their applications that they freeze, stuck in the thoughts of "what if I don't get in?" or "what if it isn't the right college for me?" Make sure you are both taking deep breaths and managing the anxiety that naturally comes with navigating high school and the college application process.

What if Your Student Doesn't Get into Their Dream College?

First of all, if a student really has a dream college, I always support them applying to it…even if I am pretty sure that college would be in the "beyond reach" category. We discuss the average GPAs, test scores, and general student profiles for admitted students. These statistics are widely available on the college's website. It is something that you can sit down with your child and do their high school freshman year so they understand exactly what is needed to be competitive at that college. We also discuss the odds of them getting in based on a variety of probability charts. But they have to apply.

My favorite story on this topic is about an amazing young man who had set his sights on Stanford University. He had been doing all the right things. He had an impeccable GPA in the International Baccalaureate program at a large public high school. He was engaged in his school and community, had demonstrated leadership skills, and was a varsity athlete. He also had a great sense of humor and basically had a profile that made him a contender at any highly selective college. His multi-page resume teemed with excellence and activity. And his essay was excellent. He applied for early acceptance to Stanford and was rejected. He was visually deflated when he told me the news. We talked about it for a long time, and I was able to convince him that, for whatever reason, his profile just didn't fit what they were looking for this year. "Fit" is the keyword here. Last year or next year, he may have gotten a different letter, but this year we had to carry on and see where else would fit for him. We then turned to his other applications. I remember to this day when he showed up in my office to tell me that he had gotten his acceptance to Yale. We also talked about the fact that Stanford could still be on his dream college list for graduate school. Sure enough, four years later, he shows up in my office with a big bouquet of roses…he had just gotten his acceptance to a two-year graduate program at Stanford University. I will never forget the young man's smile that day. The route to his dream school had been four years longer than he had planned initially, but he got there.

PART II

———————————

WHO ARE YOU?

PARENT ALERT: If you have been doing the previous exercises with your child, this part of the high school parenting experience will be much easier. Answering these questions yourself and sharing them with your child can be bonding. Not only are they the kind of questions that you need answers to for college admissions purposes, but they are also important to think about for work interview purposes. Some of these questions are very similar to the questions your student will be asked during their application process. Some of the questions are just to help your child figure out who they are and what they want to do with their lives.

CHAPTER 7

"WHO ARE YOU" BRAINSTORMING EXERCISE

The following assignment is for your student to fill out. (By the way, this can be a great exercise for you as well to share your story with them!) Junior year is probably the best time to do this exercise. These questions may take some time to reflect upon, not rapid-fire answers. Ask them if they are willing to review it with you when completed.

Assignment: Develop a 30-second "elevator pitch" or "commercial" about who you are to present to your family. Imagine that you are a "product" and that you want the admissions director at your dream school to know all about your unique "features" and how those "features" are going to "benefit" that university.

Consider the answers to the following questions:

My three SUPERPOWERS* are:

1.

2.

3.

*A superpower is something that you do and are recognized for doing with excellence. Everyone has excellence in them.

The three MOST IMPORTANT EVENTS in my life story are:

1.

2.

3.

Three words I would use to describe me are:

1.

2.

3.

Three words my parents would use to describe me are:

1.

2.

3.

Three words my sibling(s) would use to describe me are:

1.

2.

3.

Three words my best friend would use to describe me are:

1.

2.

3.

Don't guess on the three sets of words above…ask them.

If you had to give a speech right now, what three things would you feel most comfortable talking about?

1.

2.

3.

What are your three most favorite memories?

1.

2.

3.

What has been the hardest thing that you have accomplished in your life to date?

What accomplishment are you most proud of?

What is your greatest victory?

What discovery have you made that has thrilled you?

What do you spend most of your time outside of school doing?

What is the funniest thing that has ever happened to you?

What have you done that people say couldn't be done?

When did your mind and body feel in perfect harmony?

What object or possession holds the most meaning for you?

What relationship holds the most meaning for you?

What thought wakes you up in the middle of the night?

What is the last thing you think about before you go to bed and the first thing you think about when you get up in the morning?

What are you passionate about?

What surrounds you in your room...on your walls, desk, bookshelf, bedspread, nightstand, floor, backpack, water bottle?

If you have just met a stranger, what would be the three most important things that you would want them to know about you?

1.

2.

3.

In your spare time, what websites do you like to visit? Which social media accounts do you follow? What TV programs do you watch? What books do you read? What movies do you like to watch? What music do you listen to? What events have you attended and enjoyed? What museums have you enjoyed visiting?

My favorite book is?

My favorite line from my favorite book is?

If you had just worked for 10 hours at a car wash and earned $100, what would you do with the money?

What is the one new thing that you want to learn how to do this year?

If you were applying for a job at a tutoring center as a tutor, what would you want to tutor? Why should they hire you?

Where have you traveled? What was the biggest thing that you learned from your traveling? If you haven't done much traveling, where do you want to go?

If you had a free day to do anything you wanted...besides napping...what would you do?

What is your dream job? Why?

What is the most important thing going on in the world today?

What or who has surprised you the most in a positive way over the last year? Why?

What does your college roommate need to know about you before you meet them?

What one event from history do you wish you could have been present for?

The one thing I wish I could change in my life is?

The one thing that I wish will never change in my life is?

Success means? I demonstrated this success when:

Character means? I demonstrated character when:

Resilience means? I demonstrated resilience when:

Leadership means? I demonstrated leadership when:

What do you believe in?

Who is your hero and why?

What is important to you?

What are the consistent themes that are present in your answers to these questions?

Share your biggest epiphany from this exercise with your family.

The answers to the above exercise cannot only be used to help craft answers to that basic question of "WHO ARE YOU?" but can also help answer essay questions for college applications.

> **PARENT ALERT:** Helping them to begin to figure out who they are by the time they graduate from high school is part of the job of being a parent. It takes years to accomplish and will continue long after they leave your home. But, getting them thinking about what is important to them needs to be done now.

CHAPTER 8

APPLICATION ESSAY FAVORITES

Let's take a moment to talk about those college application essays as they are very, very different than you might expect. They are not a retelling of activities or big, fluffy statements that could be written by anyone. They are extremely personal examples of who you are. Over the years, I have read hundreds of application essays. These are a few of the most impactful and memorable ones I have read:

1) A young man who was accepted to Stanford University who was a state champion baseball catcher and Wendy's National High School Heisman finalist with a three-plus-page resume wrote about how he had started his love affair with chemistry and research when he went to the dump with his grandfather and stumbled across a chemistry set.

2) A young lady who was accepted to Bryn Mawr College who wrote about learning how to spit on stage while performing the part of a goat shepherd in a Shakespearean play at her high school.

3) A young man who was a part of a very large high school's International Baccalaureate program who wrote about helping to raise his sister who was 12 years younger than him. He recounted sacrifices he had gladly, selflessly made to grow with her.

4) A young man accepted to the University of Colorado Boulder who wrote about his shoelaces and how, after being a part of a wilderness camp, had never looked at them quite the same way. During his time in the wild, he had to use them as "ropes" to pitch a makeshift tent.

5) A young lady accepted to Columbia University who was 5 foot, 10 inches tall and wrote about putting on 4-inch heels and walking across a Girls State stage in a spotlight to deliver a speech.

6) A young man who was accepted to the University of San Diego who had become addicted to video games after his father died while he was in high school. He had attended a wilderness addiction boot camp where he was given the graduation nickname of White Bamboo: strong but flexible.

7) A young lady who was a national record holder in her sport of 12 years who was accepted to Stanford University and wrote about what camaraderie meant to her.

8) A young man who was accepted to Yale who wrote about building a tower of marshmallows and toothpicks.

9) A young woman who was accepted to Columbia who wrote about reading astronomy magazines while waiting in the wings to go onstage of a professional musical theatre company.

10) A young woman who was accepted to just about every college she applied to who wrote about a piece of rock that had been given to her by her grandfather that was actually a piece of the Berlin Wall. She wrote about what he had taught her about the value of freedom and how she had used his lessons in her life.

11) A young lady accepted to Dartmouth who found courage and fearlessness behind a microscope.

12) A young lady accepted to multiple Ivy League schools who wrote about learning how to speak Spanish from a snail.

The key to all of these essays was that they had concrete, believable examples that reflectively "showed" who they were. They didn't just "tell" the reader who they were; they were able to SHOW them who they were through things they had DONE while in high school. They had participated in sports, became part of the theatre community, been a part of research, valued and spent time with grandparents, read, participated in Science Olympiads, joined speech and debate clubs, spent time outdoors, learned a second language, and showed resilience in the face of tragedy. None of these things necessarily took great amounts of money to accomplish. The point is that, while in high school, these young people explored, persevered, and did things that helped them know who they were. They had values. They had found a purpose. They worked hard.

All stories were very genuine and very personal. In a variety of ways, they help the reader know who the writer is beyond a GPA and a test score. They were memorable. They also were not on topics that most students would have chosen to write about. Talk with your child about their epiphany moments of change and growth. Help them think about what they have done.

Powerful first sentences are also important. A few of my favorites from some of the students accepted to Stanford University many years ago include:

"I have old hands."

"I change my name every time I place an order at Starbucks."

"As an Asian-American, I am forever bound to the hyphen."

"The bumper sticker I placed on our family car proclaims 'SISU.'" (The Finnish word for GUTS.)

All of which compel the reader to want to read more…

PART III

LESSONS LEARNED

CHAPTER 9

I WISH SOMEONE HAD TOLD ME

In interviewing parents, these are the things that came up time and time again as to what they wish they had known before their child started high school.

I wish someone had told me that...

1) GPA and rigor of study rules when evaluating options after high school. That determination of how rigorous a high school curriculum will be can start as early as middle school. Make sure your child knows that school is their number one job.

2) Depth of passion and demonstration of that passion can be as important as breadth. For elite and highly selective college admissions, push for your child to become world class at something. Being well rounded, but they also need to be world class at something.

3) Leadership is an important skill to demonstrate while in high school.

4) Use your summers wisely…not just for vacation.

5) College application deadlines are much earlier in your senior year than you might imagine.

6) Make sure your child is taking the correct college admission test for their abilities (ACT vs. SAT).

7) Each child's voyage through high school can be extremely different with just a slightly different set of classes, teachers, and counselors.

8) What was true for you when you were in high school has NO resemblance to what the requirements are today.

9) Your high school counselor may be unreasonably overburdened with a workload that can be three times the national recommended average. In Arizona, the public high school counselor's student load is approximately 600 to 1. The national recommendation is that the workload be 200 to 1, which is still a daunting number. Your high school counselor may be drowning. Don't depend on them alone to get your child into college. Their biggest focus may be on getting students to graduate from high school. Graduating from high school and attending college are two different things.

10) Resting does not increase options…DO STUFF.

11) There is a BIG difference between being a friend and being a PARENT. Being a PARENT is much harder. Sometimes you can be both, sometimes you can't.

12) If your child has special needs, the high school may not freely and readily supply them. You may have to fight for them. The extra resources you are requesting for your child costs them money, and they may need to be convinced by you. There are people who can advocate with the school to get what your child should be receiving if they aren't listening and are pushing back. These advocates are not lawyers but know the laws of your district and the right words to use to make them provide legally required resources. Be a tiger parent in those instances.

13) Don't ignore middle school.

14) Resume building starts in high school.

15) Don't be shocked at how involved you need to be in your child's high school journey.

CONCLUSION

LEARNING HOW TO BE A SUCCESSFUL PARENT FROM A CANADIAN GOOSE

Some of my biggest, most lasting lessons in life have come from nature. I learned what it truly means to be a successful parent from watching a Canadian goose in Minnesota. It was spring, and our backyard was buzzing with newborn critters, including a mother Canadian goose and her new goslings. They had decided our backyard had the best green grass on the block, and the mother goose was allowing her six newbies to encircle her within about a three-foot radius and eat on their own. She had her back turned to the small pond behind our property and was herself enjoying our lawn. She must have heard a small rustle in the grass as a weasel approached from behind her with the very discernible intent of grabbing one of her babies and scurrying away with it for dinner. In a lightning flash, she made one of the loudest, most terrifying sounds I have ever heard, and in a single motion, she threw her wings out to her fullest extent. She looked three times bigger than she actually was and swept all six of her babies behind and underneath her. She then literally went up on her tiptoes and stretched up her neck to make her appear as tall as possible. From a distance, she looked six feet tall. Still stretching up, she bared her puffed out chest to the weasel while still bellowing and began to switch from defensive to offensive while avoiding the weasel's gnashing teeth. With the babies now as safe as they could be, she was willing to sacrifice herself for their safety. She began to stretch her neck forward and peck at the weasel, who had lost his advantage of surprise and quickly decided to leave. But not before venturing for a side attack, which was met with the mother goose quickly maneuvering her hidden brood around to avoid his advances and snarling teeth.

What I saw was a parent who was allowing children independence under a watchful set of eyes and ears, but who was ready to protect them at all costs, including with her own life if need be. In less than a second, she went from an idyllic Sunday afternoon, picnicking in the park with her little ones, to defending them with every inch of her life. I think somewhere, somehow that is the heart of what it means to be a successful parent. Protect, allow independence, and encourage growth. As their minds and judgements and impulsivity develop over time, sometimes we may end up protecting them from themselves as well as outside dangers. That first step of being a successful parent is to know what to ask, listen for, and do.

If you remember nothing else from this book, heed the clarion call to get your children off their electronic devices, off social media, away from the TV, and get them to DO stuff, to LEARN stuff, to CREATE, and to READ in an active, engaged, obsessive, deep way. HELP them find wonder and develop curiosity in the world around them. SHOW them how. Help them find that thing that will hold their fascination for life. Work to help them be the best they can be by learning who they are, embracing their weirdness, creating high but reasonable expectations, encouraging exploration and curiosity while trusting and verifying along the way. Help them see the big picture of high school and how their decisions impact an option-creating or option-limiting future. It all starts in middle school.

Their job is to learn, read, create, mature, and do. They need to move from just memorizing information to being able to take that information and analyze it. And by the time they reach their senior year, they need to be approaching a point in their learning where they can actually develop original thought and independent learning skills. If you believe, and can get them to believe, that they can be anything they want to be and that the sky is the limit (or, better yet, that there is no limit), then they will be launched. And you will have unlocked the secret to being an awe-inspiring, successful high school parent.

PART IV

RESOURCES

Sometimes teens and families need professional help. If you find yourself in this situation, the best thing you can do for your child and your family is to reach out for additional support. I have worked with students who wrote college admissions essays about their experiences with substance abuse, eating disorders, addiction, cancer, Asperger's, self-harm, coping with a parent with early-stage Alzheimer's disease, family bankruptcy, domestic violence, suicide, rape, death of a loved one or friend, criminal speeding tickets, being photographed for pornography, gender transitioning, depression, coming out, totaling a car, accidentally killing someone or permanently injuring a friend, experiencing racial discrimination, anxiety, bullying, and parental physical abuse. They all came from families where you would **_NEVER_** have guessed or imagined that the student was dealing with such adult issues. Some had parents who would have been considered pillars in their communities. These were children with child-level coping skills having to deal with very adult situations. Certain life challenges require advanced adult coping skills and an advanced experience base that teens just do not have yet.

Make sure you are ready. Talk to them. Listen to them. Spend time with them. Believe them. Show them. Keep them busy. Encourage them. Get them help when needed.

Mental Health Resources

Parent Stress Line

Parent Stress Hotline – 24/7

- 1-800-632-8188

National Parent Helpline

- 1-855-427-2736

Parental Stress Helpline – Family Paths

- 1-800-829-3777

Substance Abuse

Al-Anon/Alateen

- 1-888-425-2666

National Council on Alcoholism and Drug Dependence

- https://www.ncadd.org/

Substance Abuse Hotline (resource for youth to call)

- 1-800-662-4357

Substance Abuse and Mental Health Services Administration

- 1-800-662-4357

Marijuana Anonymous:

- www.marijuana-anonymous.org

Cocaine Anonymous:

- https://ca.org/

Narcotics Anonymous :

- https://www.addictioncenter.com/treatment/12-step-programs/narcotics-anonymous/

Comprehensive Addiction Programs Inc.:

- https://rehabs.com/

Alcoholics Anonymous:

- www.aa.org

SAMHSA – Substance Abuse and Mental Health Services Administration:

- www.samhsa.gov

Video Game Addiction

- https://www.addictioncenter.com/drugs/video-game-addiction/

Social Media Addiction

- https://www.addictioncenter.com/drugs/social-media-addiction/

Anxiety

- https://www.psychologytoday.com/us/blog/the-moment-youth/201911/anxiety-in-teens-how-you-can-help

Crisis Text Line

- www.crisistextline.org
- Text HOME to 741741

Self-Harm

Self-Injury Foundation: 24-hour crisis line

- https://www.crisistextline.org/topics/self-harm/#what-is-self-harm-1
- Text HOME to 741741

Self-Harm: Cutting

- www.selfinjury.com
- 1-800-DONTCUT

Depression and Suicide

National Suicide Prevention Lifeline

- 1-800-273-8255
- Crisis Text Line: Text Hello to 741741

24-hour National Suicide Crisis Hotline

- 1-800-SUICIDE

HOPELINE (Trained Volunteer)

- 1-800-442-4673

HOPELINE (Teen-to-teen peer counseling)

- 1-877-YOUTHLINE

National Alliance on Mental Illness

- 1-800-950-6264

Depression and Bipolar Support Alliance

- 1-800-826-3632

Talk Space App

- https://www.talkspace.com/

Very Well Mind

- https://www.verywellmind.com/

CrisisChat

- 1-800-273-8255

Grief Support

Grief Counseling

- https://www.talkspace.com/

Hello Grief

- https://teenlineonline.org/yyp/hello-grief/

Anti-Bullying

Stop Bullying

- www.stopbullying.gov

The Cybersmile Foundation

- www.cybersmile.org

Kids Helpline

- https://kidshelpphone.ca/urgent-help
- 1-800-668-6868

Bullying Support

- www.Thatsnotcool.com

Love and Respect

- 1-866-331-9474

Sexually Transmitted Diseases

Sexually Transmitted Diseases

- https://www.healthline.com/health/sexually-transmitted-diseases

CDC National AIDS Hotline

- 1-800-232-4636

LGBTQ+ Support for Teens

LGBTQ Youth Resources

- https://www.cdc.gov/lgbthealth/index.htm

The Trevor Project – CRISIS

- 1-866-488-7386
- www.trevorproject.org/get-help-now
- Text START to 678678

LGBT National Help Center

- https://www.glbthotline.org/
- 1-800-246-7743

Eating Disorders *(Be particularly mindful of female and male athletes and dancers)*

Eating Disorder Recovery Online

- www.edrecovery.com

National Association of Anorexia Nervosa and Associated Disorders

- 1-888-375-7767
- https://anad.org/

ANRED

- www.anred.com

Abuse

RAINN (Rape, Abuse, and Incest National Network)

- 1-800-656-4673
- www.rainn.org

Childhelp National Child Abuse Hotline

- 1-800-422-4453

Domestic Relationship Abuse

Dating Violence Information Line

- 1-800-897-LINK

Pornography/Prostitution

Children of the Night

- 1-800-551-1300

Physical Abuse

National Domestic Violence Hotline

- 1-800-799-7233

National Child Abuse Hotline

- 1-800-4-A-CHILD

National Sexual Abuse Hotline

- 1-800-656-HOPE

RAINN

- 1-800-656-4673
- www.rainn.org

Childhelp National Child Abuse Hotline

- 1-800-422-4453

Runaway Support

National Runaway Safeline

- 1-800-786-2929

Faith-based Family Support

Focus on the Family

- www.focusonthefamily.com

Jewish Family Service

- www.jewishfamilyservice.org

Teen Life

- www.teenlife.com

General Crisis/Youth Support

Covenant House Nine-Line

- 1-800-999-9999

YouthLine:

- 1-877-968-8491
- Text teen2teen to 839863

TeenLine

- www.teenlineonline.org
- 1-800-852-8336
- Text TEEN to 839863

Academic Resources

College Funding

Funding Resource for College/Vocational School

- 1-800-USA-LEARN
- 1-800-4-FEDAID

Need-Based Aid for College Form (FAFSA)

- www.studentaid.gov
- 1-800-433-3243
- 1-800-557-7394

College Scholarship Sites

- www.fastweb.com
- www.scholarships.com
- https://pages.collegeboard.org/scholarship-search
- www.raise.me

Book Suggested Reading Sites

- www.pulitzer.org
- https://thegreatestbooks.org/
- www.goodreads.com/shelf/show/high-school-reading-list

Scholastic Arts Competition

- www.artandwriting.org
- www.nationalportfolioday.org

Check out National Portfolio Day offered by leading arts colleges usually in October. Your high school art teacher may be able to tell you more about it as well. They can also be helpful in developing the arts portfolios.

Community Service Awards

- https://www.presidentialserviceawards.gov

Driving Resources

- https://www.healthychildren.org/English/ages-stages/teen/safety/Pages/Teen-Driving-Agreement.aspx

Leadership

Leadership can be one of the most difficult areas for your child to develop experience and is a skill that is looked for by director of admissions for college and future employers. For potential activities for your child to help them develop leadership during high school, the following are some nationally recognized programs:

1) Economics for Leaders – Foundation for Teaching Economics (FTE)

2) The Leadership Institute – Brown University

3) Students Today Leaders Forever

4) Young Entrepreneurs for Leadership and Sustainability – University of Florida

5) National Leadership Challenge Weekend – University of North Georgia

6) Usdan Leadership Institute for the Arts

7) Leadership in the Business World – Wharton School of Business

8) National Student Leadership Conference: Mastering Leadership

9) Leadership Seminars – University of Notre Dame

10) HERLead – Ann Taylor Leadership and Community Service Program for Women

11) Keystone Clubs (high school), Torch Club (middle school) – Boys and Girls Clubs, bgca.org

12) Summer Seminar – USNA
   Especially important to look into if you are interested in attending the Naval Academy

13) Summer Leaders Experience – West Point
   Especially important to look into if you are interested in attending West Point

14) Summer Seminar – Air Force Academy
Especially important to look into if you are interested in attending the Air Force Academy

15) AIM Summer Program – Coast Guard Academy
Especially important to look into if you are interested in attending the Coast Guard Academy

16) Women's Community Service and Leadership Program – National Charity League

17) Leadership and Innovation – Disney Imagination Campus

18) Growing Leaders

19) Boys Team Charity – Community Service and Leadership

20) Girl Scouts/Boy Scouts

21) Future Farmers of America

Other military-related programs include:

1) STEM Summer Camp – Society of American Military Engineers

2) Summer STEM – Naval Academy

3) Sea Cadets

4) Civil Air Patrol

5) Junior ROTC – high school program

Many local colleges and community colleges will have leadership programs for high school students that can be attended during high school summer breaks. Many local organizations also hold leadership-building activities through mayoral offices, faith-based organizations, and business associations like Junior Achievement and their JA National Student Leadership Summit. If you are looking for a way to connect with nature and start a new club at your school, you can visit www.discovertheforest.org for information on local parks near you. There are also leadership opportunities that exist within high schools through becoming a class officer, becoming the leader or officer of a club on campus, newspaper editor, tutor, creating your own club, starting your own business, etc.

There are some great books for teens on leadership development:

- *Leadership for Students: A Guide for Young Leaders* by Frances A. Karnes, PhD and Suzanne M. Bean, PhD
- *Developing Teen Leadership: A Practical Guide for Youth Group Advisors, Teachers and Parents* by Dan Appleman
- *Everyday Leadership* by Mariam G. MacGregor, MS

Community Service Organizations

This is an area where there are many, many opportunities. Ideally find opportunities that are consistent with your child's stated interest areas. As an example, if your child is interested in becoming a veterinarian, have them volunteer at the zoo, your local animal shelter, an animal rescue and rehabilitation site, etc. A virtual volunteer site that can be helpful is www.volunteercrowd. com . Other national community service organizations include:

1) Project C.U.R.E.

2) American Red Cross Habitat for Humanity

3) The Humane Society

4) Key Club

5) Meals on Wheels Best Buddies

6) Sierra Club

7) DoSomething.org

8) National Charity League

9) Boys Team Charity

10) Feed My Starving Children

11) American Cancer Society – Walk Leader

12) American Diabetes Association – Walk Leader

13) American Heart Association – Walk Leader

14) Alzheimer's Association – Fundraiser Leader

15) Junior Achievement

Local science centers and art museums can also be great places to look for leadership programs.

Research Opportunities

Many students who are interested in healthcare-related fields look for research opportunities while in high school. Some research opportunities have restrictions on age, meaning the funding source may require all people working on the project to be at least 18 years old. If you have a college or university in your area, they may have research project opportunities for you. Pharmaceutical companies in your area may have opportunities. Some hospitals may have opportunities. Below are a couple of possible resources for research projects for high school students specifically.

Research Opportunities

- https://www.scholarlaunch.org/
- www.pioneeracademics.com

ACKNOWLEDGEMENTS

During my 12 years as co-owner at Scottsdale Education Center, I had the great honor of working with many amazing families and learned so much from all of them. My first thank you must go out to them for sharing their time and secrets and concerns and wisdoms with me. I couldn't even begin to list you all. Special thanks go to Deana Aller, Linda Torkelson, Sheryl Ross, Marcy Ross, and Jessica Kulish.

Equally enlightening were my interactions and lessons from an often undervalued population of teachers and counselors in the greater Scottsdale area. Good teachers are godsends. They are the rock stars of our time. Being a good teacher is a special skill that takes training, patience, and great heart. Some who taught me the most poignant lessons include Josh Pantier (P), Allison Bogner, Marian Campbell, Adam Kohnen, Rob Gwinn, Christina Murray, Dr. Jeff Kalb, Bob Daiello (Dr. Bob), Mrs. DeFay, Mr. Weser, Mrs. Vogt, Mrs. Sherry, Mr. Wilkens, Mr. Slovis, Brad Rutkowski, Mr. Compton, Mr. Norris, Jenny Kaiser, Adrienne Jones, Ms. Hartmann, Tyler Knox, Mrs. Krumwiede, Suzy Kuhlman, Tanya Myers, and Jordan Young. You are all amazing educators.

Great thanks also go to my children. I am so proud of you. You are each accomplished, centered, loving, and loved. Think BOLD, Trust in the Lord with all your Heart, and always touch the "Butt." I know I was not perfect, but I hope you know how much I love you.

To my husband, thank you for believing in me and making this a reality. I love you. Over 35 years and forever.

Finally, great thanks to the Paper Raven team including: Morgan, Karen, Darcy, Amanda, Joy, Jesus, Rachela, Alyssa, and Gabrielle, who helped bring this book to life and Austin Rubben for cover design.

Send In Your Story!

I'm looking for great stories to include in a future book and on my website. I want to know your story.

If you have a story about how this book helped you or your child in a positive way, please tell me.

If you have a parenting tip that you would like to share and a story that goes with it, please tell me.

If there is something you learned that you wish someone had told you before your child started high school, please tell me.

Please send me your tips and stories by going to:
www.parentsareyouready.com.

To find out more information on services and programs provided by Kim and David Duckworth and Bridge Education Center, please visit: www.parentsareyouready.com

Bring *Parents, Are You Ready?* to your organization!

Kim and David Duckworth present to teams and organizations, including schools, school districts, companies, and nonprofit organizations, on a variety of topics for both parents and students. Presentations can be conducted virtually or in person.

College Admission Services

Kim and David Duckworth are available on a limited basis to meet with individual parents or students for college admission services, including college resume building and creation, college selection, essay and supplemental essay writing, interview preparation, letter of recommendation strategy, and timeline development. These interactive sessions are available virtually on an hourly basis.

Parental "Sanity Check" Services

Do you have specific questions about guiding your child through middle school or high school? Are you feeling unsure about how to direct your child to help them multiply their options after high school? Do you wonder how you can make your student competitive for elite private high schools or colleges? Is the gap year something your child should be considering? Should they be looking at community college instead of a four-year college program? Kim and David Duckworth offer virtual individualized support to parents on an hourly basis.

"Are You Ready?" Training Programs

An online workshop and workbook directed toward parents and students who are interested in getting the most out of the high school journey can be purchased on the website: www. parentsareyouready.com.

Share This Book!

Bulk pricing for book and workbook purchases may be available.

AUTHOR'S BIO

Kim Duckworth is a graduate of Stanford University where she received her BA in Communications Journalism. She was the first woman in her family to attend college. She worked in Sales and Marketing for IBM in Silicon Valley and White Plains, NY for over 10 years. She has called Arizona her home for the last 25 years. Currently, Kim is an independent college admissions coach and member of the National Association for College Admission Counseling. She personally consulted with over 7,500 high school families as the co-owner of Scottsdale Education Center (a college preparatory center) for over 12 years. She's been married 35 years, has three daughters and three grandchildren. She enjoys hiking, Labrador retrievers, reading, travel, and Telluride, Colorado.

Lightning Source UK Ltd.
Milton Keynes UK
UKHW021844170222
398853UK00010B/2282